Urban Church Planning

Walter Kloetzli and Arthur Hillman

URBAN
CHURCH PLANNING
the church discovers its community

FORTRESS PRESS

PHILADELPHIA

Foreword

The purpose of the church is the same today as it was a decade ago or a century ago. It is the same in country or suburb or teeming city. It is to bear witness to the gospel in word and in deed. It is to call men to faith, to nurture them in faith, and to help them express their faith through loving service. That purpose does not change.

But the methods for achieving it change with every age and with every situation. The pattern of yesterday will not fit tomorrow. The pattern of the village church does not fit the city congregation. We may wish that it were not so. Nevertheless we are coming to realize more and more that it is that way.

The single worship service at 11:00 A.M. was adapted to the village with its rural hinterland and the problem of morning chores. Varied schedules in the city call for multiple services at different hours. The beautiful pastoral imagery of the New Testament has to be adapted and explained if it is to become intelligible and meaningful to the apartment-tenement dweller who rarely sees "lilies of the field," knows precious little about "sheep," and understands even less about seed that "yields thirty fold, sixty fold and a hundred fold." The fundamental questions: Who are we? Why are we? How much do we count? Does God care?—these are all still valid, but they must be answered in the language of today's world of apartments, swing shifts, fringe benefits, time payments, and television. Youth programs have little meaning in urban neighborhoods where nearly everybody is over eighteen, or in suburbs where everybody is over twenty-one or under ten. Our illustrations only hint at the many complexities and suggest a few of the many adjustments necessary to ministering effectively in a modern city parish.

Church leaders are asking, "How effective are we?" Some wonder if we are effective at all. In view of the tremendous changes taking place in urban America during the past decade we have become especially concerned about our city churches. Once we thought we had great churches in the city. Now we are not sure. Some great churches of the recent past are now problem churches, struggling to survive.

How effective are we? The Department of the Urban Church of the Division of Home Missions of the National Council of the Churches of Christ in the United States of America touched off a chain reaction of inquiry in 1955 by sponsoring the Conference on the Effective City Church. Reaction to it indicated that the time was ripe for inquiry, and many studies have followed in the wake of that conference.

There has been reason for concern. Often the church has become an institution seeking to perpetuate itself without questioning whether it was fulfilling its divine purpose. It has been a healthy experience for the church to be forced to examine its degree of effectiveness and to reassess its program in the light of current and rapid urban change.

The Division of American Missions of the National Lutheran Council, through its Secretary for Urban Church Planning, has given concrete attention to these problems insofar as the churches associated with the Council are concerned. The secretary's inquiries have been greatly facilitated by the vast social and economic research information already available, and he has made good use of this information.

It seems quite appropriate that he should collaborate with one of America's recognized sociologists in this analysis of

Urban Church Planning. The book should serve as an aid to pastors and lay leaders in the congregation, as well as to denominational and synodical leaders and officers, in helping them to understand what is happening in the cities of America and what is happening to the churches in the face of urban change. It suggests how churches can analyze their situation and adapt their programs so as to further in word and deed their witness to the grace of God in Christ.

The self-study approach has been developed by many urban church leaders as a means of ascertaining past and present effectiveness, and as a device for guiding churches to even more effective service in the future. Walter Kloetzli has been one of the leaders in the development and use of this technique. Arthur Hillman, coauthor, has served as consultant in the related sociological analysis. The suggestions offered in these chapters have been followed and they have been found helpful in many churches.

We know that this volume will be informative to every reader. We trust that it will inspire many to examine anew the task and role of their home congregation in relation to the needs and opportunities in the community where it serves. Girded to serve in relation to need and opportunity, the church may effectively call men to faith, nurture them in faith, and send them forth to loving service in the church, in the community, and in the world.

                                            H. Conrad Hoyer

Preface

The growing concern in recent years for the urban church, together with the significant developments in the fields of city planning, urban renewal, and community organization, have suggested the need for this book. Information and understanding gained from the self-studies of hundreds of city congregations have further encouraged its writing.

The authors are well aware that the subject matter treated briefly in these pages is so massive that many people feel sure that we have essayed an impossible task. It is hoped more will agree, however, that a concise account of the developments in urban sociology, community organization and planning, the congregational self-study process, and urban church developments, written from a sociological perspective, will serve a useful purpose.

This book is addressed to readers with various kinds of interests. The seminarian may find it helpful as an introduction to the urban ministry, and as an aid in gaining an understanding of the challenge which it presents. Members of congregational auxiliaries might find in this text considerable material for topics and group discussions at meetings. Board members and other elected leaders of urban congregations will find here a guide for their deliberations concerning the future programming and planning of their congregation, whatever their situation might be.

Pastors and other key leaders in urban congregations can acquire from this text an interpretation of the dynamics of change in their immediate community as well as in their gen-

eral urban area. Then too, there is spelled out a step-by-step
self-study process for the individual congregation to conduct
by itself or in conjunction with study committees from neighboring congregations. Bibliographical references are provided
to facilitate further study. The many suggestions for thought
and action are intended to encourage continuing attention to
these fields.

The book calls attention to the need for adaptations in city
church programs in the interest of making them more relevant
to the needs of people in their changing neighborhoods. However, it is hoped that others will develop further practical suggestions for meeting specific needs, and appraise even more
fully the current experiences of various urban churches. Intensive investigations, such as the Urban Church Effectiveness Study conducted by the National Council of the Churches
of Christ in the United States of America, will be basic to further thought on programming.

On the one hand, this book may be read by anyone interested in learning more about the general developments,
problems, and opportunities of the city church. On the other
hand, it can serve as a manual to guide congregational committees in an actual analysis of their congregation and community. A suggested reading and meeting schedule for those
doing a self-study is outlined in the Appendix.

One can only acknowledge generally, but gratefully, the
part played over the years by students, colleagues, congregational study committees, urban pastors, home mission
leaders, city planners, and urban renewal leaders, all of whom
have helped to develop the point of view here expressed. Appreciation is due to the various staff, committee, and board
members of the Division of American Missions of the National Lutheran Council, the Department of the Urban Church
of the Division of Home Missions of the National Council of

the Churches of Christ in the United States of America, and others. Our special thanks go to Mr. James Mason and Miss Doris Hoel for their excellent assistance and counsel in the preparation of this work. Permission to reproduce excerpts from works mentioned in this book is hereby gratefully acknowledged.

Walter Kloetzli
Arthur Hillman

Contents

1

The Growth of Cities

The rise of modern America is the rise of her cities—the economic and cultural centers of her technological age. Built by countless hands, by the men and women who have come here from all over the earth, the American city towers as the massive symbol of a nation's material achievement and wealth, as an engineering wonder, as an amazing wilderness of the dreams and works of man. Indeed, to understand America, one must understand her cities.

Here is the world of the elevated, the skyscraper, and the subway; of packing houses, freight yards, docks, steel mills, mail-order houses, universities, television studios, and churches of every creed; of open markets and streets of banking, congested alleys and shaded residential avenues; of furnished rooms to rent, brownstone houses, houses of glass, parkways and boulevards, white ghettos and black ghettos. Here is a world of neon, stone, and steel, an ever widening household of overflowing millions. Not all have taken the journey to the city, it is true; yet few are removed from the force of its impact and its way of life.

Metropolitan America

Urbanization—the growth and spread of large cities and of an urban way of life—in the midst of geographical spaciousness, is perhaps one of the more significant features of the American scene in recent years. To many observers it has seemed unusual that the United States, a nation of majestic mountains, vast open spaces, and broad rivers and valleys, should be essentially an urban nation, known for and dominated by its cities and their great concentrations of people. While most of the larger nations of the world have a greater number of people per square mile, few have larger proportions of urban population than does the United States. The 1950 census reported that well over half of the nation's population lived in cities of fifty thousand or more, or in the densely settled fringe areas adjacent to these cities. Yet these same centers of population, or metropolitan areas, covered but 7 per cent of the total land area of the United States. This concentration in or near cities of fifty thousand or more is striking enough, but metropolitan growth on a gigantic scale is indicated by the fact that in 1950 fourteen of these metropolitan areas had a population of over a million. Together these supercities accounted for one-fourth of the nation's total population.[1]

The trend toward urban living, on the increase since the mid-nineteenth century, has been most marked in the past fifty years. This is the same half-century that has also seen the continuing decline in rural farm population (16.6 per cent of the nation's total in 1950, as compared with 34.9 per cent in 1910[2]). There has been in the same period a steady growth of the older cities of the northern and eastern states, a rapid

[1] Donald J. Bogue, "Urbanism in the United States, 1950," *American Journal of Sociology,* LX (March 1955), 471; Special Committee of the Board of National Missions of the Presbyterian Church in the United States of America, *Report on the Study of the Inner City* (1956), p. 8. Hereafter cited as *The Study of the Inner City.*
[2] U. S. Bureau of the Census, *Statistical Abstract of the United States, 1955* (Seventy-sixth edition) (Washington: U. S. Government Printing Office, 1956), p. 13.

acceleration of city growth in the South and West, and the rise of brand new cities and numerous suburban communities within the outer belt area of central cities. Between 1900 and 1950, while the population of the nation nearly doubled, the population of its urban territory, which includes by census definition all cities of over twenty-five hundred population, more than tripled. Within this same half-century 73.2 per cent of the total population increase of the United States was claimed by cities of fifty thousand or more and their metropolitan areas.[3]

Most important in the urban trends of recent decades has been the growth of the areas surrounding the metropolitan cities. Here the population has grown more than twice as fast as in the central cities themselves. With the conclusion of World War II the suburban trend, which had come into its own in the early twenties, suddenly became a boom. The picture of the city as a hustling metropolis fringed only by its quiet suburbs and their rural neighbors was transformed into the panorama of people, houses, factories, expressways, parking lots, drive-in theaters, churches, motels, schools, and shopping centers sprawling into the countrysides, seemingly without pattern. Expanding as they are, the great cities of today are actually becoming regional cities or extensive urban areas. Because of their spread outward along relatively narrow belts of traffic linking city with city we now have in the making "strip cities," new patterns for the metropolitan America of tomorrow.[4] In the process, drastic changes occur not only in the rural surroundings into which the cities are spreading, but also in the centers from which they have grown.

[3] Donald J. Bogue, *Population Growth in Standard Metropolitan Areas, 1900–1950* (Housing and Home Finance Agency, Washington: U. S. Government Printing Office, 1953), p. 14.
[4] *U. S. News and World Report,* March 2, 1956, pp. 37–40.

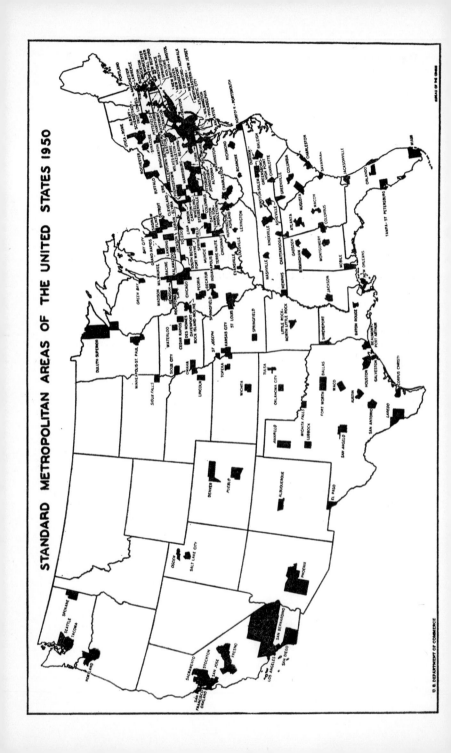

STANDARD METROPOLITAN AREAS OF THE UNITED STATES 1950

U. S. DEPARTMENT OF COMMERCE

BUREAU OF THE CENSUS

The changing form of the city

The development of the outlying regions of the city is not the result of mass exodus, but rather of an overflowing of the city into its surrounding territory. It is part of the steady growth of the city outward from its central core or original settlement. As the city has spread, its changing form has been determined by its geographical location, by the kinds of activity that have marked its history, and by the movements of people within its borders. While appearances may give other impressions, the city's growth has not been altogether pattern-less. Today, for example, the design of the city's outward spread is very much influenced, if not controlled, by the ever present motor vehicle, which in recent years has increased in number at five times the pace of population growth.[5] In earlier decades the patterning of city growth was as often determined by the routes of public transit, and still earlier by the walking distance to the central places of buying and selling, of work and worship.

The structure of housing within the cities shows similar changes in pattern and design, influenced by the ongoing development of new building materials, changes in the techniques of construction, and the development of such later necessities of mass living as central heating and the electric elevator. Because of the rapidity of the population increase in the cities, however, and because of the consequent expansion of cities over such a relatively brief span of time, cities

[5] Joseph C. Ingraham, "Autos in Urban Regions Rule and Frustrate Living," *New York Times,* January 28, 1957, p. 1.

There are 168 standard metropolitan areas in the United States according to the 1950 Census Bureau report. Such an area includes the county containing the central city or cities of 50,000 population or more, together with the contiguous counties which contain a preponderance of nonagricultural workers and a high diversity of population, and which are socially and economically integrated with the central city.

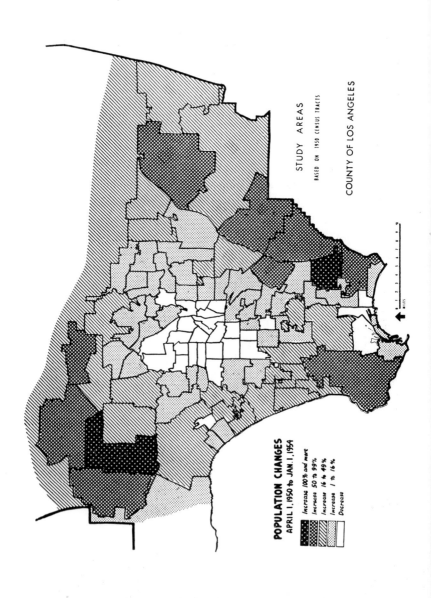

POPULATION CHANGES
APRIL 1, 1950 to JAN. 1, 1954

Increase 100% and more
Increase 50 to 99%
Increase 16 to 49%
Increase 1 to 16%
Decrease

STUDY AREAS

BASED ON 1950 CENSUS TRACTS

COUNTY OF LOS ANGELES

MILES

often afford only the impression of haphazard and formless design. The styles, forms, and patterns from many eras of city growth all seem to remain side by side within the one collective mass. Within a generation the demands of motor traffic are forced upon streets originally built for pedestrians and horses. Within a decade the demands of concentrated mass living are brought upon outworn houses originally built for spacious town life.

As the city grows, its land comes to be devoted to a multiplicity of uses—factories, stores, churches, schools, parks, houses, streets, and railways—and in the process visible patterns of land use are developed. Industrial activity, which tends to be located along routes of traffic and transportation, is often most heavily concentrated toward the central area of the city, at the focal point where transit and traffic within the city generally converge. Commercial activity, centered in the "downtown" of the city or central business district, tends to move outward from this center along the main thoroughfares and find secondary centers in the outlying residential areas. Residential growth similarly moves outward from the center. Often the oldest dwellings are those located near the area of original settlement. In many cities, these residential areas near the city's center have seen a constant stream of successive residents. The residential history of these areas can often be told in terms of an unfolding of population growth in the city, from the original citizens to the most recent inhabitants. An area of rapid change, of deterioration and blight, this central core of the metropolitan area, with its mixture of land uses, its nearness to railroads and industry, and its years

Each study area (group of adjacent neighborhoods) is rated according to population growth. The darkest areas had the highest percentage increase. The next darkest areas had a more gradual population growth. The areas that are without markings actually had a population decrease. The greatest population growth in metropolitan areas occurs at the periphery.

of poor building maintenance, is often the very area into which the most recently arriving, low-status population finds its homes and its initiation into the life of the metropolis.

Cities within cities

Larger cities are often a vast conglomeration of many separate residential areas, all intermingled with the other land uses of the city. Some have developed with the expanding city as pockets of residential settlement; some through identification with a particular economic, racial, or national group; and some as outlying communities recently swept into the city in the wake of its growth. Some of these areas have distinct boundaries, either the natural barriers of hills and waterways or the man-made barriers of railways, broad expressways, industrial zones, and commercial streets. The boundaries of some are defined by barriers of class and color. Others have no distinct boundaries, but are simply those sections of the city of which its residents speak with familiarity and loyalty as "the neighborhood."

Many of these residential areas within the city are recognized by their own unique features, features that are often dear to the residents themselves, such as the topography of the area, historical monuments and churches, the nature of the houses, or the layout of the streets. Many other areas are recognized by the peculiar interests of the residents, by the nature of their work, and even by their age and sex composition. Some sections of the city are marked by class distinctiveness, such as those sections housing the older families of the city and those of upper economic and social status. Many other districts, growing as racial and national islands and often expanding into wide areas of the city, are recognized by their people, their shops, or even their language: the city

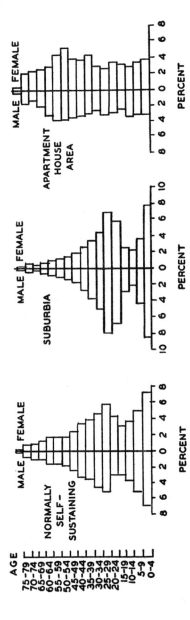

Population composition varies from one neighborhood of a city to another. These population pyramids describe the composition of various neighborhoods. The length of any bar to the left or right from the center of the pyramid indicates the percentage of the total population in that neighborhood which falls within a certain age range (male population to the left; female to the right). Each step in the pyramid represents a five-year age increment—the lowest, 0–4; next, 5–9; then 10–14, 15–19, etc.

worlds of a Bronzeville, a Polonia, a Greek colony or a Little
Tokyo. There are areas of the city in which there is a notice-
able preponderance of Catholic churches, or of Lutheran
churches, or of synogogues, which indicate the religious heritage of the residents. In other areas, Episcopalian or Congregational churches might be more predominant, and in still other
districts of the city gospel tabernacles and storefront missions
mark the religious climate of the community.

While many of the "cities within the city" are able to keep
their distinctiveness for several generations, many other communities and neighborhoods might change within a generation
or less. Smaller cities are likely to have a more homogeneous
population, perhaps through the influence of a single dominating industry or a single racial or national majority. Here
neighborhood changes and movements of population may not
be as evident as in the larger city. The larger city is a composite of many populations, and its changing patterns of residential living are likely to follow the patterns of changing
population groupings.

Where do all the people come from?

As one walks through the streets of the city, or as one surveys the tables of population growth in cities, no more natural
question could be asked than this: "Where do all these people
come from?" In recent years, the growth of cities has been
due more to natural increase—the excess of births over deaths
—than to the moving in of people from other countries or from
rural areas. In the 1940-1950 census decade migrants to the
cities of the United States, millions as they were, accounted
for less than a third of the population gains of urban areas.[6]
The gain through natural increase comes from the reversal of

[6] Bogue, "Urbanism in the United States, 1950," *op. cit.*, p. 474.

a previous downward trend in the birth rate. It was so low
during the mid-1930's that in the cities it was below replacement level. Since the late thirties there has been a marked rise
in the birth rate, and it has remained high compared with the
earlier low point. That this is more than a temporary phenomenon is indicated by the increase in the number of third and
fourth children born to the same mother.[7]

Natural increase alone, however, cannot account completely
for the growth of cities, particularly in their times of rapid
rise. Historically, the main source of city growth has been in-
migrants—persons coming to the city from other regions. In the
earlier decades of the rise of cities a considerable portion of
urban increase, especially in the northern and northeastern
sections of the country, was due to the successive waves of immigration from abroad. Some national groups, it is true, were
more attracted to the soil than to the fortunes of the city, yet
many others, despite rural backgrounds, remained predominantly in the city. This was true of the Irish in the first period
of immigration and it was notably true of the later immigrants from eastern and southern Europe. The fact that Cath-
olicism is the majority faith in many of the larger cities of the
country, and that Judaism is essentially an urban phenomenon
in America, has its roots in these periods of immigration when
thousands came from beyond the sea. Today, with the closing
of the gates of entry to the New World through restrictive
immigration laws, what was once a flood of immigration into
the city from abroad has become a mere trickle, composed
largely of refugees from eastern Europe and of fellow Americans from Canada, Mexico, and the West Indies.

While the decline in foreign immigration to cities has
meant the diminishing of a once-important source of urban

[7] U. S. Public Health Service, *Vital Statistics; Special Reports,* XLII
(December 21, 1955), 13.

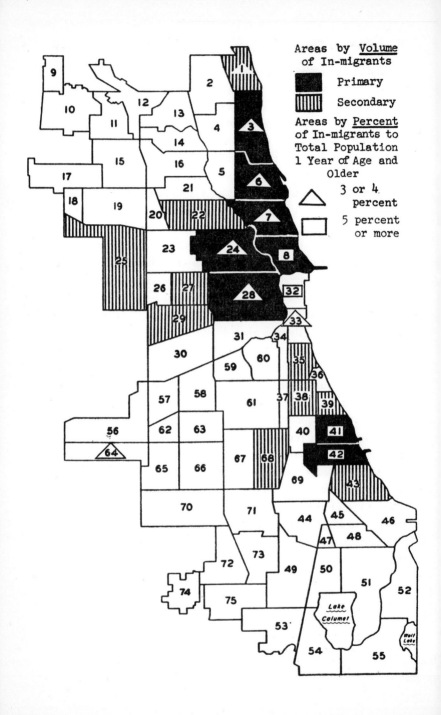

Areas by <u>Volume</u>
of In-migrants
■ Primary
▥ Secondary

Areas by <u>Percent</u>
of In-migrants to
Total Population
1 Year of Age and
Older
△ 3 or 4 percent
▢ 5 percent or more

population increase, there has been no diminution in the lure of the city. As in the past, from the Yankee migration out of the hill country of northern New England into the rising inland cities of early nineteenth-century America, on to the movement out of the Dust Bowl in the thirties into the cities of the Far West and Southwest, and right up to the recent migration out of the marginal farmlands of the South into the industrial cities of the North and of the expanding Southland, the American city continues to draw upon the human resources of its own territorial hinterlands. Not unlike those newcomers from rural Europe of a century ago, today's newcomers to the city—the American Indian, the southern mountaineer, the Puerto Rican or the southern rural Negro—are often unfamiliar with the ways of metropolitan life. For many of these, carrying with them the centuries-old traditions of rural life, an adjustment to the world of the city is difficult enough in itself. Yet it is made even more trying because of the barriers of prejudice with which they must also contend.

Striking in the recent migration to cities has been the growing proportion of nonwhites (a census designation including Negroes, Indians, and other nonwhite races) who are moving into urban areas. Nonwhites in cities increased from 6.5 million in 1940 to over 9.5 million in 1950. During this same period, while only 10 per cent of the urban population is nonwhite, over 44 per cent of the net in-migration was nonwhite.[8] Patterns of segregated residential housing in many cities have meant that most of this increase in urban nonwhite population has been in the central cities rather than in the suburban or fringe areas. In some areas where residential segregation is

[8] Bogue, "Urbanism in the United States, 1950," *op. cit.*, p. 477.

The dark community areas had the highest rate of in-migration. The striped areas had the next highest. The northern concentration indicates white port-of-entry areas whereas the southern concentration generally speaking represents nonwhite port-of-entry areas.

most rigidly enforced, not necessarily by law but by the agents of prejudice, increase in housing for Negroes has lagged far behind the increase in Negro population. The result has been that Negroes must continue to pile up within relatively small areas of the city, areas already too crowded for adequate living arrangements. In earlier periods of the history of American cities many immigrants were able to improve their positions economically and socially and to move away from the inner city areas of their first settlement. The Negro, however, in following this same route, meets with more resistance if not actual violence.

Families on the move

The growth at the edge of large cities, the natural increase of city population, and the continuing migration of people into the cities from rural areas and from other cities, have meant extensive changes within the cities, yet changes which have been a part of the American urban scene from its beginnings. Change, in fact, is the style of the city. Among the familiar sights in any city are the scenes of change: buildings coming down and new apartment houses rising out of the rubble of tenements, lots for sale, homes being built, rooms for rent, moving vans on the street—all indicative of families on the move. While there are millions each year who are movers into the city, there are millions more who are movers within the city itself. In the period 1955 to 1956 alone, over twenty million city dwellers, one out of every five persons living in cities, moved at least once during the year. Of these, nearly 14.5 million were moving from other locations within the same county.[9]

[9] "Mobility of the Population of the United States: March 1955 to 1956," *Current Population Reports*, Series P–20, No. 73, pp. 1–4.

The movement of people within the metropolitan area is very much a part of every block and every neighborhood. Accelerated by the recent wave of prosperity, the increasing mobility trends are not without their serious effects in all sections of the city, including even those relatively stable communities where residents have long taken a pride in their local institutions, their churches, home ownership, and their own long attachments to the neighborhood.

Many move when their neighborhood begins to change or is threatened by a change in the composition of its population. They leave when people of a different racial or national background come into their community in search of better housing or more adequate space than was afforded in some former crowded quarters. In such cases, it is all too often an entire neighborhood on the move, churches included. Some move in order to seek residence nearer their place of work, particularly as industrial districts and shopping centers are developed farther from the center of the city. Others move because of changes in marital status or in employment. Some move to find better community facilities, such as parks, playgrounds, or schools for their youngsters; others, to find more space in which to spend their increasing leisure hours. Many, perhaps the greatest number, move in order to find better housing accommodations to meet the changing needs of the family or to find more satisfying surroundings for their family life.

Areas of the city with a high percentage of movers, a high rate of mobility, are usually those which immediately surround the larger institutions of the city, the university neighborhoods and furnished-room districts, those areas in which there are many young white-collar and professional workers or a high percentage of young people generally. However, the highest percentage of movers, the largest proportion of new residents, is usually in those outer edges of the city into which the city is expanding, and in those districts nearest to the city's core.

Those areas of the city nearest its center, near to the port-of-entry into the city and in the midst of congested industrial, commercial, and traffic concentrations, have long been described as highly mobile areas. This core of the city is characterized by cheap hotels, rooming houses, dilapidated dwelling places, and mixed land uses. Its transient populations move through buildings long worn by the succession of former residents and through districts long marked by the effects of social instability and confusing change. Spreading from this center even into the outlying reaches, and following in the wake of the expanding metropolis, is the inner city, that deteriorating inner core of the city with its most visible characteristic being that of physical blight and decay.[10] While the impact of families on the move may be felt by churches across the city, it is in the inner city particularly that the effects are grave indeed for the urban church.

The changing city

The accelerated growth of cities, expanding without precedent into the countrysides; the rapidly changing form of cities, today styled to the pace of the motor vehicle; the shifts in population composition; the increasing movement of people within and between cities, the characteristically American phenomenon of mobility; the physical changes evident within inner city areas—all describe the changing scene of contemporary metropolitan America. The effects of this changing scene have been many. City neighborhoods which have seemingly changed overnight in their composition, and rural hinterlands

[10] *The Study of the Inner City.*

which as suddenly have become colonies of commuters—of industrial workers and laborers as well as of white-collar workers—have both meant significant shifting within the urban community: shifting of political loyalties, of school needs and requirements, of religious backgrounds and interests, even of traffic patterns and shopping habits.

Invariably the changing city has created problems for local governments: problems of fire protection, water supply, health and safety, sanitation, law enforcement, education, physical planning, and public welfare. Besides heightening these concerns in many cities, the rapidity of change, together with the expansion of the city beyond its borders, has accentuated the problem of governmental jurisdiction in the wider urbanized area.

Nor have churches been spared readjustment in the wake of the changing city, as can be seen in the new churches appearing daily within the outer ring of the growing city and the older churches of inner city areas closing their doors as their congregations move away. Important as have been these physical and population changes occurring across the breadth of metropolitan areas, perhaps more important for the churches have been the effects of the new way of life—a style of life characteristic of the urban citizen of the changing city.

It is true that the cities of America are wonders in themselves—the rich products of enterprise, imagination, and human decision. Yet above all else the city is still a household and a dwelling place, a massive gathering of persons, each involved in the thousand complexities of the urban way of life. From the streets of outworn tenements and frame houses, through the endless avenues of the outlying neighborhoods and into the shaded walks of the most distant suburbs, the truism is everywhere demonstrated that "the city is its people." The oldest families and the native sons of the city, the immigrants from abroad and the in-migrants from rural areas, intercity movers and families on the move within the city, the schooled and the unschooled, the churched and the unchurched—these are the makers of the changing city. These are the creators of the style and the form of the changing city, and of the urban way of life, a way which has become increasingly the way of modern man.

2

The Urban Way of Life

Beneath the spectacular facade of the city skyline there are more subtle factors which add up to the urban way of life. The adjustment to this new life on the part of persons moving into it from rural areas reveals in a striking way the qualitative differences in social and personal relations which exist within the city, differences not always realized by the city dweller himself.

The newcomer in the city

Not only is the rural in-migrant often moving into an entirely new and unfamiliar landscape in which the natural surroundings of country life are replaced by the man-made structures of the city, but he is also moving into sometimes drastic changes in the nature of his social relationships, in the structure of his family life, in his standing among his fellows, and in the rhythm of his work and the routine of his day. His lack of acquaintance with the countless facets of city life—from public transit facilities and schedules to garbage disposal and rental collection—and his encounter with the endless variety of people and of things in the city can be overwhelming to the newcomer from rural areas.

Even those institutions familiar to him from his former surroundings—stores, schools, and churches—operate and look differently within the urban setting. His encounter with these institutions might often be a completely new experience for the in-migrant. He might find, for example, that even the church of his own denomination is quite different in its city setting from what it was in its rural setting, different in its worship, in its program, and in its fellowship, as also in its welcome to the newcomer. Not feeling "at home" in the company of such a congregation, and lacking a sense of "belonging" even in the church of his own denomination within the city, the newcomer may readily strike out to find other kinds of religious fellowship, including very often the store-front sect, or, as more often happens, he can drift away from any religious affiliation at all.[1]

For the newcomer, the diversity within the city may itself be an advantage to him as he seeks employment, residence, or amusement. At the same time, the bewildering choices it affords him may be a big disadvantage as he moves from job to job, from house to house, or from one amusement to another, never finding close identification with any of these facets of city life. The isolation which the newcomer feels may be made even more extreme by barriers created between himself and his city fellows on account of his language, color, or lack of urban sophistication. In time he might find, within the city, pockets of neighborliness in which he can again strike roots. Yet memories of his own past, lived in the natural, more intimate surroundings of a rural life, often continue to be his dearest treasure; in his isolation, or in moments of sensitive reflection, his longings may well turn to his past. While city life may never be able to fulfil such longings, the economic advantages and the relative freedom it affords can easily take their place, especially as the newcomer advances into levels

[1] J. Milton Yinger, *Religion, Society, and the Individual* (New York: Macmillan, 1957), pp. 167–168.

of acceptance measured by such symbols of status as dress, an automobile, and a home.

While the effects of new urban surroundings may be trying to many newcomers, the effects upon their children may be even more drastic. The need for the security of strong roots and for the stability of home and community life often is not met in the careers of recent in-migrant children. The frequent failure of the city and of its institutions, including churches, to meet these needs, as well as to facilitate the adjustment of the rural newcomer to the city and its way of life, has its result in the delinquency and general social disorganization that have increasingly become the mark of in-migrant areas. Certainly the impact of urban life is seen in its full force in the problems which the rural in-migrant and his children have to deal with. Meanwhile the native moves in accord with the city way of life, not even realizing how much its features contrast with those of a rural setting.

The world of the city-dweller

The congestion of city life and activity, the mass of traffic, the clatter and noise, the crowds of persons and clusters of buildings, the insufficiency of space, the great diversity of people, activities, and things—these are popularly supposed to characterize the world of the city dweller. The consequences of these physical conditions are likely to be much more profound than it may appear on the surface. The effects of crowding, especially in the housing of low-income groups, are not limited merely to the hindrance of rest and the added exposure to disease. There is also the lack of opportunity for that personal development which space, privacy for study, and the development of hobbies would otherwise make possible. The consequences of a remoteness from nature may include a diminishing appreciation of the natural processes of life and a possible loss of any understanding of man's own affinities with them. Certainly the crowding, the clutter of city life, and the host of stimuli constantly confronting the city dweller have their serious effects on his daily life. They involve costly expenditures of energy and often produce strain and irritability. The desire of city dwellers to remove themselves from these and other effects of the physical conditions of city life is evident in the prevailing movement outward in residence—toward the space and quiet of the outlying parts of the metropolitan area—as well as in the streams of week-end traffic moving out from the city into the country.

The city dweller is played upon by a variety of stimuli. He has many selections to make, whether it be on a shopping tour or in choosing recreation or other activities. A visitor to the city knows of the multiplicity of points of interest and places of amusement. A newcomer to the city likewise may know of a multiplicity of jobs possibly available to him, from which, with fortune, he may be able to make selective choices. Churches, too, afford choices to the city dweller. Just as he may visit many shopping centers or many places of amusement so also he may visit many churches in the task of selecting a church home.

Not unlike most portions of the industrial and technological world, the urban citizen's household, garage, and place of work or amusement are filled with an array of mechanical gadgets, contrivances, and mechanisms, with most of which he has but a superficial, knob-turning acquaintance. To the city dweller, such a state easily becomes enlarged to include even a goodly portion of the scene about him. Subways, elevateds, sanitation systems, elevators, traffic control systems—these and the many other necessities and familiar features of urban life are understood by their users only in their form and in their use, although the same body of users is dependent upon these necessities throughout their daily lives. The urban dweller is actually dependent upon a host of specialists, experts, and technicians, with few of whom he has any direct knowledge or acquaintance. This is a striking illustration of the separation, the alienation of the city man from the processes and makings of his own surroundings.

The size of the city and its complexity, as a gathering of persons in which thousands are active daily in their patterns of work, of schooling, of recreation, or of shopping, necessitate the organization of movement within the city—and organization of time and routine. Time clocks, stop lights, school calendars and church schedules are necessities within the city. Each reveals something of the strict routines within which city people pass their lives. The size and extensiveness of the city also have consequences in the scattering of a city dweller's affiliations across the geographic spread of the metropolis. He often has long journeys to work, to school, to church, to places of shopping, to friends, and to relatives. Yet spread across the city as his affiliations and loyalties may be, his movements between places are movements very often controlled by the restrictions of urban routine.

For many the effects of routine include not only exhaustion, but also boredom and feelings of aimlessness, of being "caught on the treadmill" or "tied to the machine."[2] For many, as well, the effects of routine include more than irritability; there is even a deep-seated hostility toward work and everything connected with it. The routinization of life is not without its effects upon churches either. To many city dwellers church attendance and participation is but a supplement to the routine of the week, a segment of personal life quite sep-

[2] Erich Fromm, *The Sane Society* (New York: Rinehart, 1955), pp. 103 ff.

arate from the other activities and affairs of daily and weekly life.

The city as a gathering of persons

Just as a city person is often familiar with a diversity of objects, goods, and institutions, so also is he often familiar with a diversity of persons—of a variety of backgrounds, concerns, vocations, and points of view. The urban dweller is often exposed to a greater variety of human situations and human beings than is the citizen of the smaller, less heterogeneous community. The cosmopolitan air of the city gives hearing to all shades of political ideologies, religious affiliations, and social points of view. The city dweller is often within hearing distance of them all, even if seldom more than superficially aware of the implications of what he hears. Because of this diversity, the city often provides a person with the opportunity to find kindred spirits among his fellow citizens and the stimulation of association within a community of shared interests, as witness the colonies of artists and musicians, or the array of associations within the city.

While the city dweller encounters a greater variety and number of persons in the course of his daily activity, his relationship to these persons tends to be superficial, hasty, even cautious and guarded. In spite of the larger number of persons about him the urban citizen may have even fewer intimate relationships with other persons than do members of the smaller or rural societies. His travel, his shopping, his amusements, and even his work are often carried on in the midst of total strangers. So, too, might be the nature of his religious associations. Despite all the concentration of people, there are in the midst of the turmoil of cities many people who experience a peculiar kind of loneliness. The nearness of many people and the number of contacts with them are not personally satisfying and may even accentuate feelings of personal isolation.

Leadership and authority in cities tend to become remote and impersonal, often creating distrust of political leaders and those in authority. This actual distance between populace and leadership may, in fact, create more opportune situations for civic corruption, or for the replacement of civic responsibility with apathy, than is always possible in the smaller political unit. The ordinary voter or householder feels overwhelmed by the bigness and complexity of his city. And this makes it easier for concentrations of power to form.

Although people in cities are dependent upon a larger number and a greater variety of persons, there is a lesser degree of dependence upon particular persons. Dependence in urban societies is more upon the functions of persons than upon the persons themselves. So too persons are recognized not so much by name or character as by the functions which they perform. Beyond their functions and their uniforms, the persons themselves remain, despite their wide and varied contacts, simply the anonymous persons who compose the mass fabric of urban society.

The greater concentration of persons in cities, the wider diversity of persons, and the anonymity characteristic of this concentration and diversity afford a degree of freedom which for many has been part of the lure of cities, drawing people into their ranks. Cities, for example, have long been known as the centers where the arts have flourished, and where people with imagination and with competence in intellectual skills have gathered. While the relative freedom of cities has spawned its misfortunes, its maladjustments, and its isolation of persons without sense of tradition and without roots, it has also bred a rich heritage of creativity and intellectual curiosity. It is often, however, a tribute to the strength of the individual when under urban conditions he achieves individuality and distinctiveness in the face of the pressure toward conformity.

Coupled with the industrialism and technological developments of recent centuries, urbanization has also been accompanied by, and through its relative freedom of life has even partially encouraged, the emancipation of women, youth, and the aged. It has also fostered change in the pattern of kinship ties and of family structure.[3] Although this is not unique to urban life, the urban family is increasingly one in which loyalties are primarily to spouse and children, and only secondarily to wider kinship structures. The urban family is expected to provide for the basic personality needs of its members. Its cohesiveness does not depend on economic production or other functions performed by families in agricultural settings. As a result, a greater emotional intensity is evident among the members; some families are much more cohesive even than in days past. While the seeming rootlessness and mobility of persons within the city may give impressions of disorganization carried into all levels, yet the appearance of the urban core family gives an example of the possible stability that can be attained within the complex changing surroundings.

A considerable portion of the mobility of persons within the city is actually keyed to the movement of family units, not to that of isolated individuals. The popularized version of the middle-class family, arranged about the living-room watching television, is not an unrealistic picture of family life as idealized by the present urban age. The emotional intensity of family relationship, however, means that the breaking of

[3] Harold L. Wilensky, "Changing Patterns of Family Life," *Children,* III, No. 5, (September–October, 1956), 163–69.

family bonds may carry with it an even greater intensity of emotional shock. It may also mean that marriage bonds will be more readily broken if they do not produce the affectional response or the "happiness" expected as a right. The effects of these changing family patterns may be severely felt by the senior members of the wider kinship circle, including grandparents, especially as it becomes evident that they are not expected to follow along with the younger members as they begin to establish their own families. Finally, the emerging urban family pattern may require a drastic adjustment on the part of those families from rural America and from foreign parts whose traditions of courtship, family authority, marriage, family structure, and kinship loyalty may be in conflict with most of the corresponding traditions they inevitably encounter in an industrial, urbanized society.

In the large-scale organization of metropolitan communities there are enough people and a large enough variety of interests to result in a specialization of associations and institutions to an extent which oftentimes staggers the imagination. There are agencies and groups organized for every conceivable purpose—recreational, educational, cultural, as well as the maintenance of memories and loyalties to colleges, home states, nationalities, and cultural or national heroes. Along with the larger groupings of service, fraternal, patriotic, labor, and commercial associations and auxiliaries, these too have their positive side in providing a basis for community in voluntary association. But they also tend toward a compartmentalization of activity among persons related to the various groups and associations. For many, the spread of these associations across the city, over and above work and family affiliations, can mean an even further exaggeration of this kind of separation of responses and activity. In this too, church membership and participation is not excepted. Indeed, the possibility of keeping even that segment of a person's life separate from all other parts is enhanced under urban conditions.

Diversity and standardization in the city

Diverse are the backgrounds, the points of view, the prob-lems, and the vocations of city people. Diverse too are their affiliations and loyalties. Often the only seeming sem-blance of integration in the city is its routine—its day shifts and night shifts, its traffic signals, its daily and weekly sched-ules. Having no common tradition, no common ground of thought or of religious expression, the city community assem-bles a set of values which, beyond mere routine, becomes the common ground for its citizens. In the American city, a ma-terialistic ethic has become just such a common ground. The measuring of its citizens is a measuring keyed to those visible symbols of this ethic: income, property, dress, and the auto-mobile. While the city dweller may not share political opin-ions or religious feelings with his neighbor, he does share with him an involvement in the same economic system, whether he accepts that system or not.

While the symbols of status associated with this economic system are almost always a significant part of social class dif-ferentiation, an understanding of social class within the diversity of the city must also emphasize the broader and more subtle factors in class difference. The type of work, observ-able public behavior, the many variations in speech and in social skills, habits of caring for property, recreational pat-terns, preference for type of church service, are all associated more or less with class differences.[4] It follows that any change upwards in income, or even the stability of income, is in itself

[4] See studies of social class by W. Lloyd Warner and associates. See also J. P. Marquand, *The Point of No Return* (Boston: Little, Brown, 1949).

not enough to effect a quick change in class position. Under mobile and relatively anonymous conditions of social contact, these distinctions may be hidden at first glance by the kind of clothes or car a person has. Wherever there are opportunities to know people more than superficially, however, these differences are recognized, if only unconsciously. Suburbs often have a greater homogeneity, which is associated with a defensive pride in maintaining their class "quality." The struggle to maintain and improve social status is not as evident in large cities as in some smaller communities, including outlying suburban communities, because in the large city people can be less aware of their competitors. Nevertheless there is in a broad way a consciousness of class alignment.

The association of persons, representative of the diversity of the city and of the range of social classes, is vividly seen in the mingling of people in the vehicles of public transportation. Here, in this company of total strangers on their way to any of the variety of activities in the city, persons are recognized by their most visible features—their badges and their uniforms, be they white collars or blue collars, gray flannels or a policeman's overcoat. The mingling of persons and social classes in subways or buses, in the traffic of streets or in sidewalk crowds, does not imply a similar mingling across the city. Patterns of neighborhood segregation and of community barriers within the city enforce the rules of class differentiation. Likewise, places of amusement, eating places, voluntary associations, and churches are very often identified by class. Churches, for example, may often be readily recognized as belonging to a certain social class. As a result, the church's membership may steadily decline when the former class group moves away, while any other group is reluctant to move in because of the class connotations of the church.

Although there are many churches closely identified with

a certain racial, national, or class grouping, there are many other churches which reflect the very diversity and heterogeneity of the city itself. These churches, not unlike the public schools of the city, often find themselves in the position of adjusting to a common denominator of service in the community. Churches are often found to gear their appeals to the average member of the average congregation; they adjust their religious education, worship, and program with the idea of reaching the most people through an economy of effort and space. Public schools, likewise, face the constant problem of providing challenging opportunities for the exceptional child, and of counteracting in other ways the effects of mass education.

The standardization of life evident in many schools and churches is seen even more clearly in the mass political appeals and mass advertising campaigns of radio, television, and newspapers. Through these primary media of communication within the diversity of the city the effort is made to reach larger numbers with an appeal geared to the tastes and interests of what is conceived to be "the average man." The pressures toward conformity are often extreme in suburban communities and in the expanding white-collar and professional occupation groupings.[5] But they are also felt across the breadth of the entire city, although in varying degrees and expressions. There are different ideas, in the shop, at church, in the bowling alley, and at the union meeting, as to what constitutes deviation from the common type. The pressures toward conformity often feed on a deep-seated longing for acceptance and for a sense of community. All this results in

[5] David Riesman with Nathan Glazer and Reuel Denney, *The Lonely Crowd* (New York: Doubleday, 1953); C. Wright Mills, *White Collar: The New American Middle Classes* (New York: Oxford, 1956); and William H. Whyte, Jr., *The Organization Man* (New York: Simon and Schuster, 1957).

a general unwillingness to separate oneself from one's fellows or one's community by advocating unpopular ideas, by speaking out on principles of moral and social action, or by doing anything from conviction that the community may possibly define as strange or unacceptable.

Part of the pressure toward conformity is that of keeping up with one's peers—"with the Joneses." Here again the visible symbols of status and approval become the measure of conformity. The actual shallowness of these symbols, rooted in the value system of urban society, may be observed in the adolescent's pursuit of the most visible attributes of this system—something noisy or flashy—as the means of achieving acceptance among his peers and recognition from the adult world. The same is true of the desire of many newcomers to the city to move toward what is thought to be social acceptance through the show of dress and automobile, even at the expense of the necessities of life.

The search for community in the city

The pressures toward social acceptance through conformity and attention to social status reflect the search for community in the changing scene of the city. The strengthening of family ties based on the conjugal relationship rather than on the traditional larger kinship structure is another result of the effort to find a semblance of community in the midst of the city. The patterning of residential areas into little segregated worlds distinguished by nationality, color, or class, and the pockets of neighborliness to be found in many sections of the city also represent facets of community feeling. A child born into the city may, in fact, grow to maturity holding fast to a rich affection for his city, treasuring his home place as much as does the child born into folk or rural society. Emphases placed on

the rootlessness or on the problem of urban life often overlook
the fact that for thousands the city in itself is a goodly inheritance and an intensely satisfying environment. Yet the
anonymity, routine, congestion, and crowding, and the constantly changing physical scene of the city and of city life do
have their serious effects upon countless other persons involved in the complexities of urban life. For these the city is
not always an inheritance to treasure, nor is it the source of
their moments of satisfaction.

Many city dwellers have lost any sense of tradition or of
having roots in the community. They have a loyalty to their
home place only to the extent that it is the place of their economic livelihood. For many the loss of roots or of a sense of tradition may be accepted as the condition for choosing a livelihood in the city. For others the loss of tradition might be replaced by closer family ties, by a more intense involvement in
work or by seeking out and finding closer associations with
kindred minds. For many others the rootlessness and frag-
mentation of the city can actually induce a sense of isolation
and loneliness.

A sense of being alone and without the support of group
relationships may often result in personal disorganization to
be seen in certain forms of mental disorder, marked by various
degrees of withdrawal from social contacts. "Delinquent" behavior may be a form of protest and rebellion on the part of
alienated people, which in turn is symptomatic of a deep conflict within society. Sometimes the aimless and random nature
of juvenile brutality is not fully understood by the youngsters
themselves. It is a reflection of their situation—a situation
which includes the very conditions of city life itself: its pre-
occupation with things, its fragmentary emotional security,
and the impersonality of its relationships.

The consequences to the church, and the challenges presented to it by these features of community identity, loss of tradition and group relationships, are many. The current revival in religion and the recent swelling of membership rosters in churches and religious institutions may be partially accounted for by the longing on the part of many to find new roots or stability within the changing urban situation.[6] Many churches have been effective in strengthening a sense of attachment and of tradition within their communities. Many others have brought new sources of strength to individuals through an outreach which speaks uniquely to the condition of people in the city.

Within the breadth of its concentrated compass and as the most significant expression of the dominating pursuits of the present age, the city reflects the predicament of personal and social life inextricably involved in the complexities of a materialistic age. To be sure, social life under urban conditions does represent a unique way of life. Yet it must also be seen as a way of life both formed and shared within the wider context of the whole modern industrial and business society—including even the farthest reaches of rural life. The city is nothing less than the very situation of modern man himself; it is his plight.

[6] Will Herberg, *Protestant–Catholic–Jew: An Essay in American Religious Sociology* (New York: Doubleday, 1956).

3

The City and the Church

"Perhaps my church is an exception," said the pastor, "but when our present building was erected some thirty years ago it was out in a literally open countryside, with nothing but a scattering of houses around the whole area. Since then our congregation has gone through the new residential influx and experienced a suburban boom. After that came a period of steady growth, then a leveling off. Today we find ourselves in one of the blighted areas of our city with all of the changes and problems that represents. In just three decades our church has gone from birth through life into its declining years."

Perhaps this congregation was an exception. But many congregations have experienced, at least to a degree, some of the changes and adjustments that this pastor spoke about. That we might better realize what happens to a church over a period of time, let us consider three typical city congregations that erected their buildings all in the same neighborhood.

The people contributed to the construction of their houses of worship. They wanted the church to be as near to their homes as possible. Regular attendance at worship services and frequent participation in programs and activities during the week were stressed a great deal. By thus serving its members in several ways the city church has often become the very center of life in its neighborhood. This is no doubt an oversimplification, but it does point to a social tie which many Americans have with their church which is not found in certain other parts of the world.

In a matter of a few years this particular city grew and changed; the neighborhood around the three churches became quite different. Many members moved farther out to newer areas. Those moving into the neighborhood were not like the members of its established congregations. Perhaps they were of an entirely different cultural background. Many neighborhoods which were once predominantly Protestant have been known to become almost completely Catholic or Jewish. In some instances the people moving into the neighborhood were even of a different race. The effects of race prejudice were to be felt here too.

One of these three city churches voted to sell its building to another denomination or sect that was anxious to move into the neighborhood and minister to the people. Then, with the proceeds from the sale, plus additional funds contributed by the membership, they moved into an area that was more accessible and acceptable to their members. There are many churches in America that have relocated not once but twice. One church in Chicago has relocated seven times.

But not all the churches in this position followed the same course of action. The second congregation realized that the new people moving into this old neighborhood needed the gospel just as much as, if not more than, the former inhabitants. This church made a determined stand to bear witness to its faith to all persons within its reach.

The third congregation was neither willing nor able to adjust itself to the changing community. It could not accept the newcomers, and it did not have the strength to relocate. It became one of the many city churches which have simply died out over a period of years.

"Queen and Carpenter have pointed out* that when a church is declining, its members moving away, its area being 'invaded' as a result of ecological changes, there may be a number of different responses: The church may adapt its program to the changing character of the district; seek a new location; it may disband and sell the property; it may gradually grow smaller, with a faithful few holding on in the hopes that something will happen to allow them to preserve the organization; or it may develop into a metropolitan church. Sociologists of religion have scarcely explored this situation enough to specify the variables that influence which of these various responses will be made. The type and speed of the 'invasion,' the class status of the constituency, the denominational connections, the nature of leadership are perhaps important factors."[1]

Types of churches

Just as there are different types of areas in our metropolitan centers or communities so there are different types of churches. The downtown churches, the suburban churches, and those in areas in between all tend to serve different kinds of people and to have distinctive programs.

As the vast metropolitan areas of today grow and change with the passage of time the churches located there find themselves in ever fluctuating situations. Increasingly they appear to be serving a procession of people, ministering to a migrant multitude. Each church finds itself in a different kind of position.

The downtown church is generally the church that was first

* Stuart A. Queen and David B. Carpenter, in *The American City* (New York: McGraw-Hill, 1953).
[1] J. Milton Yinger, *Religion, Society, and the Individual*, p. 294. Quoted by permission of The Macmillan Co.

established in the community by a given denomination. It is sometimes known as First Church and often spoken of familiarly as the "mother church." Chances are that its children have been scattered far and wide and that daughter congregations have been established all across the metropolitan area.

This church finds itself at the center of the metropolitan area, located in the midst of transiency, traffic, and business. Those who are not particularly rooted in a given neighborhood and whose children have possibly grown up and moved away are quite often inclined to attend it.

It often occupies a strategic location in that it sometimes serves as the voice of its denomination. Frequently it is called upon to act as spokesman for the denomination on matters of community concern. Generally speaking, it symbolizes the denomination at the heart of the metropolis. Conferences and general meetings may be held here, and it serves other churches in the community through institutes on church music, leadership training, and the like. Special church officers are often associated with it. By virtue of its strength and prestige and tradition, it often has a strong pulpit ministry. The musical program of such churches is often of a high caliber.

Because of its unique circumstances and location, this church is generally not identified with a particular class or neighborhood. Rather it reaches out into every part of the big city. The Sunday school, though not very large, does command good leadership. Advertising in hotels, newspapers, and railroad stations is a "must" for this kind of church.

Generally speaking, the population in the downtown area of the city is constituted of middle-aged and older adults living in apartments and rented rooms. There is a relatively low proportion of "familiness"—that is, many people are living completely alone, apart from any other family member. In this kind of neighborhood the community spirit, the sense of belonging, tends to be extremely low. The program of the church needs to be oriented to the "unrelated individual." Counseling is extremely important. Adult education programs have proven effective. Opportunities need to be provided for small groups of persons of like background to get together. Many variations in evangelism need to be tried and developed in such areas of the central city.

The multineighborhood or regional church is not located in the very heart of the city but is generally considered to be in the inner city area. It finds itself in a residential neighborhood which once used to be of a higher class than it is today. Now, however, the homes have been divided into apartments and perhaps even the apartments have been divided into separate rooms. Then, too, this church is likely to find that within its parish boundaries there have developed some very desirable new apartment buildings. So it is faced with the responsibility of ministering to a population which is not homogeneous.

Over the years the membership has gradually scattered to different parts of the metropolitan area. Yet the church has continued its ministry in its present location. It does not have the prestige and tradition of the downtown, or first church, and therefore tends to draw people more from a sector of the metropolitan area than from the full circle of it. Located beyond the strictly business and downtown district, this church is not strategically situated to serve the hotel and transient population of the middle and upper classes. Rather, the kind of transiency that it experiences is related to the "port-of-entry" areas and the lower levels of society.

Transportation facilities have had a marked effect on the membership distribution of this church. Bus lines, streetcars, and major arterial highways have contributed to the outreach of the church in specific directions. This type of church tends to be so committed to serving several neighborhoods that it never quite relates itself to its own immediate neighborhood. As long as the changes are not too great in the neighborhood, this kind of regional policy will not markedly affect the church's future.

The population in this general type of neighborhood tends to be older than the average for the city as a whole. There is a high proportion of middle-aged and older adults but there are also some children and teen-agers (see chapter VII). The percentage of "familiness" in this neighborhood is considerably higher than that of the downtown area yet far lower than in the homogeneous suburban area. The church in this area needs to have a program both family-oriented and individual-oriented.

The neighborhood church is the church that, either consciously or unconsciously, has identified itself with a particular neighborhood, with a specific set of parish boundaries. Such a church, by being closely identified with its community, is often involved through the leadership of its pastor and laymen in a host of community activities and responsibilities.

This church attempts to serve a geographical area regardless of the class, race, or economic make-up of that neighborhood. As the neighborhood changes, so does the make-up of the church. Most churches begin as neighborhood churches but with the passage of time often depart from this pattern. The vast majority of suburban churches can be considered as neighborhood churches.

In the older neighborhoods of the city we find these churches playing key roles in the combatting of social problems and in the strengthening of vital community agencies. Here there is need for a ministry to the senior citizens almost without exception. There is often the problem of overcrowding and inadequate housing facilities. In such areas churches are responsible for helping to meet some of the areas' needs, such as those in youth activities or neighborhood organization. Especially in the older established neighborhoods are the processes of social change at work. Congregations in these areas therefore can play a major role in the harmonious transition of the neighborhood over the passing of years. It can help the old-timers accept the newcomers.

The selective or special-group church is the type of church which, by virture of either historical developments or processes of social change, has limited its ministry to a certain part of the population. This selectivity might be on the basis of race, nationality, or class, or other factors. As neighborhoods change and its members are scattered, and as the population continues to become more heterogeneous, this kind of church finds itself in increasing difficulties. But in some cases the historic and sentimental loyalties which the members have for their church are so deeply rooted as to make it possible for the church to continue drawing its constituency from widely scattered areas.

The term "selective or special-group churches" often suggests nationality-oriented churches. For example, there are many Lutheran churches that began their ministry caring exclusively for people of German, Swedish, Norwegian, or Finnish background. But there are other types. There are those that are oriented strictly to the intellectual approach to religion, emphasizing such things as comparative religion, social action, and civic leadership. By virture of their message they attract a selected group of persons. Selectivity on a class basis is a very powerful factor in the life of many congregations.

Whatever the form of selectivity might be, it needs to be recognized and evaluated in the light of the inclusiveness of the Christian gospel. Some of these churches have deliberately chosen to restrict their ministry to these special groups. Others have tried to make the transition to a more neighborhood-centered ministry, but for various reasons have failed. Still others have actually been able to accomplish the transition.

The suburban church. It is true than some of the churches generally called suburban are quite old and well established. Obviously we need to differentiate between the newer developing areas and those suburbs that have been established for some time. Some of the churches which find themselves in the suburbs are actually very close to the midtown or old multineighborhood type of church. There are some suburban churches which are already finding themselves in slum areas. Generally speaking, however, the suburban church type refers to those congregations which have been established in recent years and which find themselves in the "bedroom" areas of the metropolitan centers, where the commuters sleep.

These churches generally minister to a homogeneous population. There are many children and young adults, relatively few teen-agers and older people. They are most often identified with their immediate parish area or neighborhood and are in the process of growth and expansion.

"Although some outlying residential areas and suburban communities near large cities have been so quickly built and poorly planned that they show signs of becoming future slums, the typical suburbs are composed of middle class, fairly comfortable people. Business executives and others with more than average income may be inclined toward some smugness, at least a feeling of satisfaction about the success they have achieved. There is both physical and social distance between them and the masses of people living modestly or precariously on income from industrial or more menial employment. The temptation is there to ask, 'Why can't those people do as well as we have done?' The homogeneity and physical well-being of suburbanites is reflected in their churches."[2]

The store-front church in various forms is to be found in the blighted "port-of-entry" areas of the American city. It springs up overnight in response to the religious and social needs of the newcomer who is usually from the rural South. The man who serves as leader or minister of one of these store-fronts is generally employed full time in some occupation and does this work as an extra. His "flock" consists of perhaps twenty-five to fifty persons from the immediate area around the store-front. The training of the minister is usually minimal; few have completed high school. A few of the more success-ful store-fronts eventually blossom into full-fledged congre-gations when they are fortunate enough to purchase a build-ing abandoned by the congregation of one of the established denominations.

J. Milton Yinger gives a good description of the thinking and the needs of the people who constitute these churches. "When a lower-class person moves from a rural area into a city, to work in a mill or factory, he is confronted with a number of difficult problems of adjustment. He is forced to accept an enormous change in his style of life—the rhythm of his work, the nature of his associations, his place in a neigh-borhood. He is likely to be almost wholly lacking in organized social contacts, because he enters the new society at its most poorly organized level. And his sense of isolation is increased by the way in which he is looked down upon by the estab-lished urban groups. This is the kind of problem with which religion might be expected to deal: You are not alone; you belong; your problems are not everlasting, or at least they have

---

[2] Arthur Hillman, "Urbanization: Its Impact on Protestantism in Amer-ica," *Lutheran World,* III, No. 4 (March, 1957), 355.

meaning in a transcendental context. But the established churches of the city are poorly equipped to give these assurances to a lower-class migrant from a rural area. For the most part they are fully accommodated to the middle and upper classes of the city—the forms of their services of worship, the content of the preaching, the programs and leadership of the various groups in the church are all adjusted to the urban members of long-standing. The lower-class sect movement then is in this situation an attempt to grapple with the problems faced by the migrant, a response to what Holt calls the 'cultural shock' that comes from the shift to an urban life, an attempt to heal the distress caused by isolation and insecurity. It is not likely to be an economic protest, at least in any direct sense. The migrant may be better off financially in the city. He is almost certainly ill-equipped by earlier training to protest against his economic status. The established churches, in fact, are probably more liberal on economic issues than are the lower class sects. Far more than an economic protest, the urban sect demonstrates the widely different personality needs and modes of expression that one finds among status levels."[3]

Impact of social forces on congregations

Studies of several of our city congregations have revealed some interesting findings, reflecting quite directly the impact of the social forces mentioned earlier. Perhaps the most startling bit of information is the cumulative effect of mobility. In other words, what happens to a city church as a result of these population shifts and changing neighborhood patterns? Our self-studies of several hundred such churches have shown

---

[3] J. Milton Yinger, *op. cit.*, pp. 167–68. Quoted by permission of The Macmillan Co.

there are very few that still have on their rolls more than half
of their membership of ten years ago. Almost without exception at least 50 per cent of the present adult membership of
our city churches have joined the congregations within the last
ten years. The American urban church can then be seen still
more clearly in the light of this information: it ministers to
a procession, an ever changing, ever different group of people
who through the years come within range of its influence for
varying periods of time.

Theologians, social scientists, and philosophers have had
much to say about the ills and the liabilities of our modern
urban culture. Not the least of these problems related to life
in the modern city is the impersonal and rootless existence
which it fosters. In I John 3:17 we read, "If any one. . . sees
his brother in need, yet closes his heart against him, how
does God's love abide in him?" It becomes increasingly difficult to be concerned about our brother's need in the city
scene because we don't see our brother. We hardly know our
brother. The very nature of urban life keeps us from knowing
him.

A rural pastor who recently began a ministry in the very
heart of one of America's largest cities made some interesting
observations. "Back in South Dakota," he said, "my people
would see one another several times a week—in numerous
social and business contacts; we really were neighbors and
knew one another. Here [in the city] my people are scattered
over great distances. It is almost impossible for me to visit
them even once in two years. My people don't see one another
from one Sunday to the next. They're strangers in almost every
sense of the word." The impact of all this upon the city church
becomes obvious: people coming and going, people who
hardly know one another, whole neighborhoods being flooded
by strangers. The church in this situation must make concrete

attempts to bridge the gap of loneliness and the prejudice which typically exists between the old-timers and the newcomers.

Studies of urban churches also call attention to the significance of lay leadership. There are numerous activities and organizations directly related to church life in the American city. The various congregational organizations elect their own leaders. It is understandable that, unless special attention is given to the mobility of membership, the leadership of the church will tend to become dominated by the senior members, those who have been members the longest. The new members do not know one another. It takes a while for them to be assimilated into the ongoing life of the congregation and become an active part of the fellowship of that church. The result is that those who have become a more integrated and cohesive group, the older members, tend to acquire more than their proportionate share of responsible offices. Leadership should really be representative. Our self-studies have shown that in many city churches, though one-half of the members joined in the last ten years, only about one-fourth of the leadership comes from them.

Another finding closely related to those previously mentioned is that of leadership distribution. For various reasons the elected leaders tend to live still farther away from the church than does the average member. Thus still another barrier is created between the people in the neighborhood of the church and the laymen elected to offices of leadership within the congregation.

Here we see, then, a series of social forces and their influence within the structure of the city churches. Isolation, detachment of members, lack of awareness, and, possibly, ultimate lack of concern for the needs of the community around the church are fostered and developed by transitions.

Thought patterns and church life

No evaluation of the urban church scene can be complete without a realistic consideration of some of the psychological factors involved. These are not as easily discerned nor can they be stated in clear-cut statistics. Nevertheless, they are very real and have a tremendous influence on the thinking, outlook, and effectiveness of our churches.

The first factor is the "middle-class" concept. This group in our society is roughly defined as that which is neither wealthy nor poor, neither intellectual nor ignorant. This concept has created in American thought a glorification of the "average" situation at the expense of sensitivity to, or awareness of, the unusual or the different (see chapter II). Even in the training of pastors the dynamics and special needs in our various types of communities (rural *vs.* urban, inner city *vs.* suburban) have been ignored so much that we have not seen the deep issues confronting anyone trying to minister in a non-middle-class or untypical situation.

Just one example will serve to illustrate this point. A young Puerto Rican mother struggling to care for her family in the teeming Manhattan tenement section in which she lives finds it most difficult even to understand the English language and to know how best to feed her children. This is such a problem with her that it comes before all else in her thinking. If the church is to bring the gospel to her it must also be concerned about this very immediate problem of hers. Specifically, then, there is a need for the American church to recognize the deadening effect of our middle-class mentality or preconceptions and to develop a sensitivity to the unique characteristics, problems, and concerns of its neighborhood.

A second factor is the "success story." This has sometimes been called the Horatio Alger or bootstraps philosophy. We have not, as a nation, learned many of those lessons which are taught by suffering alone. Our vigor and unique success have created in many minds the conception that if only we would try harder, if only we would work more earnestly, then, no matter what, we could expect to see a flourishing story of success, be it in the life of an individual or of a congregation. Many Americans unconsciously have this highly idealistic picture of what their lives, their communities, and their churches ought to be. They are so bound to these preconceived goals that they cannot see the reality of their situation.

Dietrich Bonhoeffer in his book, *Life Together,* has this to say about man and his dream of success or "wish dreams": "God hates visionary dreaming; it makes the dreamer proud and pretentious. The man who fashions a visionary ideal of community demands that it be realized by God, by others, and by himself. He enters the community of Christians with his demands, sets up his own law, and judges the brethren and God Himself accordingly. He stands adamant, a living reproach to all others in the circle of brethren. He acts if he is the creator of the Christian community, as if his dream binds men together. When things do not go his way, he calls the effort a failure. When his ideal picture is destroyed, he sees the community going to smash. So he becomes, first an accuser of his brethren, then an accuser of God, and finally the despairing accuser of himself."[4]

A third factor might well be labeled repression. This is closely related to the preceding two factors. The American who is dedicated to the middle-class way of life and is striving blindly after his "wish dream" finds reversals and failures almost unbearable. We have put a premium on the kind of

[4] Dietrich Bonhoeffer, *Life Together* (New York: Harper, 1954), pp. 27–28.

person who does not speak negatively. We buy millions of books that tell us how to think positively. We seem to believe that a person can examine himself and repent in the setting of a success story rather than by being humbled and made obedient at the foot of the cross. The American finds it difficult to speak openly and frankly about problems and concerns, about setbacks and failures. The fact of the matter is that in many of these areas of acute change, of racial and ethnic shifts of population, adjustments will be slow and painful. There will be disturbances within and without the congregation. An awareness and a confrontation of the problems and issues involved are necessary.

A fourth factor is isolation. In the *Lutheran World* for Winter, 1954, Dr. Walter Freytag mentions that one of the factors in the decline of the church in North Africa was this: "The churches obviously lacked ties to and communication with the universal church."[5] A similar situation exists in many of our inner city parishes. It must seem almost foolish to compare the isolation existing between continents centuries ago with the isolation inside modern America with its telephones, press, radio, and television. However, it is a very real issue with many pastors and laymen in these inner city congregations. The effectiveness of their witness is limited by a feeling of despair and defeat, of being cut off from the vital, active, growing areas of the church.

We discussed earlier the individual and neighborhood isolation which is fostered by the urban pattern. No doubt this isolation contributes to the parochialism and institutional self-centeredness of many urban churches. More often than not this becomes a defense, an attempt to shut out the world around them. But in doing this, they cut themselves off from

---

[5] Walter Freytag, "The Lesson of North African Church History," *Lutheran World*, I, No. 4 (Winter, 1954–55), 295.

their brethren of the household of faith. One result of this "hiding in a shell" is that pastors and lay leaders from churches only a few blocks apart are oftentimes total strangers. The feeling of being isolated from sister congregations and from the main stream of the church is very much in the picture of urban church analysis.

4

Churches and Community Planning

Individuals who are prudent make plans, both on a short-term and on a long-range basis. When we speak of planning in private affairs we mean that people set goals or objectives for themselves and consider the best means for attaining them. They have to be prepared to make revisions in the light of new developments. This does not mean that people can always regulate their lives according to a rational or logical pattern. However, personal planning does imply a sense of direction and of priority. It implies a steward-like concern about the expenditure of time and resources rather than a careless and casual approach to the problems of living.

Business firms engage in planning with regard to expansion of production facilities, extension of markets, and the recruiting and training of workers. In fact, the bigger the business the more likely it is to plan systematically. The basic idea of planning is, therefore, not a strange or foreign one. Of concern here is the fact that communities too are increasingly providing means of insuring orderly development in matters of common interest.

Orderly development

The growth in size of cities makes some planning essential if only for survival. Traffic problems often provide the main impetus. The possibilities of paralyzing congestion are so real that the best efforts of engineers and civic officials are required. Apparently less acute in large cities, but nonetheless threatening, is the rotting away at the core which is visibly damaging both to property values and to human welfare.

Plans for community development are basically the responsibility of city governments, or of municipalities in co-operation with counties or other local governmental units. The physical aspects, particularly, of city planning include the regulation of land use together with consideration of population density and the movement of people and of goods, the location of public buildings and recreation areas, and the co-ordinated development of water, sewer, and other basic services. Potentially this involves the forecasting of governmental expenditures (capital budgeting) and the determination of priorities in public works. Not all cities have a comprehensive planning program but all are forced to give some attention to these matters.

Providing for the orderly and comprehensive development of communities is more than the planning of physical facilities and of other visible arrangements. Important as these are, there is need also for consideration of community services such as health, education, welfare—those provided by government as well as voluntary agencies. In this respect too the growth of cities and the attendant variety of institutions and associations have made necessary the exertion of conscious efforts if there is to be any approximation to the degree of co-ordination and the kind of order normally taken for granted in a smaller community.

Planning is a continuous process of meeting new problems and making changes in the light of experience. A plan should not be conceived of as a rigid blueprint which thwarts healthy development. It simply provides a general framework within which the details will need constantly to be adjusted. Only thus can developments in the various parts of the city be co-ordinated. This is the object of both physical planning and social welfare planning.

There are distinct jobs to be done by the traffic engineer, the architect, and other technical specialists in planning. But the over-all determination of policy, if communities are organized democratically, is not for the experts or planners alone. Decisions must ultimately be made by governmental legislative bodies or by boards of social or civic agencies. And in the process of reaching agreement on matters of policy, there should be opportunity for citizens to raise questions and to make their wishes known. Professionals or planners on the one hand, and citizens or laymen on the other, have complementary roles to play in a democratic planning process. One hope in writing this book is that more churchmen, through greater familiarity with community planning as it is usually carried on, will be able to take part in it, not only as churchmen interested in the well-being of their churches, but also as citizens concerned about the orderly development of their communities.

The actions of property owners whether constructive or negligent, the investments made in business blocks or factories, and the locations chosen for church edifices and other community structures—these and other forces in the changing city are all the result of decisions made by many individuals and private corporations. The planning process is essentially an attempt—sometimes a fumbling and tardy attempt, it is true—to provide some "rules of the game, as it were, for private development."[1] As a function of government, planning is concerned with street patterns, public buildings,

---

[1] Gerald Breese and Dorothy E. Whiteman (eds.), *An Approach To Urban Planning* (Princeton: Princeton Univ. Pr., 1953), p. 13 *et passim.*

roads, and the like; but it is more than that. If we recognize that the major determination of the form and character of the city is in private hands, it becomes clear that to plan generally is to provide a framework and leadership for what might otherwise be a sprawling and formless growth. Change is inevitable in community life as we know it. The problem is to provide a sense of direction and of order.

Agencies for Planning

When congregations make plans for buildings or other facilities, or changes in program, either singly or on the basis of area-wide strategy, they usually need to make specialized studies of the kind which will later be described. However distinctive the policy questions they face, churches will find it helpful to work with various community planning agencies. By so doing they not only gain access to useful bodies of factual material but also learn early about projected changes such as highway routes or the rebuilding of certain areas. Pastors and lay members of church planning committees should not hesitate to turn to the kinds of agencies described below. They will usually find co-operation and a willingness to meet more than halfway those who come seeking help.[2]

City planning, as carried on by some agency perhaps called a department or a commission, is an arm of the city government. The city planning agency may have only advisory powers, or it may be given responsibility for the actual

[2] See "Planning Notes," in *The City Church*, VII (September–October, 1956), 20, for a letter from the director of planning of Los Angeles County inviting co-operation with churches. See also Walter Kloetzli, "Planning Tomorrow's Cities," *The Christian Century*, LXXIII (August 1, 1956), 898–900, and also by Kloetzli, "Churchmen Have an Important Part to Play in Urban Renewal," *The Journal of Housing*, XIII (July, 1956), 244–45. The latter article tells of co-operation between leading church representatives and of planners nationally. (Hereafter cited as "Churchmen in Urban Renewal.")

administration of zoning ordinances or the regulation of sub-divisions. Its functions are basically to do research and to provide needed technical help in such a way that various departments of the government will be inspired to turn to it confidently and with a readiness to accept its recommendations. The work is related both to the executive and the legislative branches of government. That is, it is a staff service to various administrative units and its recommendations take effect only when they have the sanction of the city council or the appropriate legislative body.

City planning is often associated with maps. Much of the work must be in just such visual form. However, a general plan or a comprehensive development program is broadly inclusive. It deals not only with geographical areas but also with standards of population density, and indirectly with the quality of housing construction. City planning attempts to give form to the city by helping determine the location of industry, residences, traffic arteries, and space for recreation and other community services. In recent years, especially in cities where there is capable leadership in the political sense and in the professional realm, the scope of city planning has been broadened. Early in the century when city planning was still a new concept primary attention was given to the layout of streets and public building sites, with special emphasis in some places on the "city beautiful." The newer scope of thinking, however, includes much more. Now there is increasingly concern as to whether the city is functionally efficient for both industry and residence, and in general whether it is an attractive place for people to live.[3]

Zoning has become generally accepted in American cities since about 1920. It is one of the major tools for implementing

[3] Christopher Tunnard and Henry H. Reed, *American Skyline* (Mentor Books, 1956); Arthur Hillman and Robert J. Casey, *Tomorrow's Chicago* (Univ. of Chicago Pr., 1953), pp. 51–52.

the general plan. Zoning does not determine what will be built in a given part of a city, but it does set limits to individual decisions. The zoning ordinance usually states that certain areas may be used only for residential, for industrial, or for commercial purposes. In each category there will be subtypes. For residential areas this means regulating the density of population by limiting the height of buildings, number of multiple-dwelling units, and so on.

For industry the newer thinking is in terms of performance, or the kind of effect that a factory will actually have. It is no longer assumed that all factories are inherently bad in a given area. The amount of noise or odors or fire hazards which are created by a plant are among the factors which determine whether it should be allowed within close proximity of residences. It is evident that some industrial buildings, with appropriate architecture and landscaping, may be far from detrimental to an area. Moreover, the location of factories is related to the amount of transportation. It is important to have them located conveniently for the people who are to work in them. In general, zoning is more than a negative measure telling property owners what they may not do. It is more properly thought of as a way of maintaining stability of property values by preventing the inharmonious mixtures of land uses.

The planning of schools and parks is closely related to the over-all development of a city. Specific responsibility for this planning may be in the hands of separate local authorities, but co-ordination is needed within the general framework of the city plan. The trend in relation to parks is to think of their accessibility and usefulness as playgrounds for children, but to some extent also as a service for people of all ages. It is generally believed now that there should be a park close to each home as opposed to the nineteenth-century conception of parks as show places for ornamental gardens and promenades. The whole matter of tax support for recreation centers is relatively new. Public planning in this respect is tied in with that of volunteer agencies such as boys' clubs, settlement houses and various organizations for youth.

Agencies providing recreation services and other agencies more easily identified with the field of social work, such as children's homes, clinics, and family and case-work agencies, have grown with the cities—beginning in the nineteenth century but most marked in the present. The diversity of specialized agencies was the result of many kinds of spontaneous action taken in response to crises in urban life.[4]

In the course of experience the separate agencies found that they needed to get acquainted and, if possible, to agree on common standards. After a period when agencies simply talked over mutual problems informally, there came the period before World War I when councils of social agencies began to be organized in leading American cities. This movement gained rapidly in the years between the wars and now councils are found in all principal cities. Agency representatives serve on council committees and boards, but in cities of any considerable size the work of such volunteers is organized and supplemented by staff members. In larger cities there may be several professional specialists serving in each functional area.

Council purposes obviously include the preventing of duplication and other forms of working at cross-purposes, as well as the co-ordinating and raising of standards of service. Councils also engage in positive planning for new services that their programs for meeting health and welfare needs may be evenly distributed throughout a city. The word "need"

[4] Arthur Hillman, *Sociology and Social Work* (Washington: Public Affairs Pr., 1956).

itself is subject to constant analysis and redefinition on the basis of new experience. Councils, which now more often are called welfare councils, include not only the voluntary agencies, most of which are supported by the community fund, but also the local governmental agencies such as relief departments, boards of education, park districts, and health departments.

Church-related agencies too participate in welfare councils but the extent of their activity varies. Churchmen are also among the board members and committee members taking part in the welfare council as a matter of civic concern, and as a means of expressing a thoughtful and systematic approach to the welter of urban problems which might otherwise seem overwhelming and chaotic. Community funds or chests include church-related agencies insofar as their work is not directly a part of the program of local congregational life. The distinction between what is a community service and what is a church program is far from a simple one, as, for example, in connection with a church-sponsored settlement house. Recent work has been done by Protestants to define the scope of their social work and to indicate the principles which distinguish them from secular agencies and government programs.[5]

Churchmen who are concerned with social action in matters of housing, fair employment, or such public issues as are part of the "wholesale" or preventive side of social work may find collective strength in working with other forces in the community. In the history of social work a broader approach is part of the tradition, particularly of the settlement house

[5] E. Theodore Bachmann, *The Activating Concern (Churches and Social Welfare, I)*; Horace Cayton, Setsuko Matsunaga Nishi, *The Changing Scene (Churches and Social Welfare, II)*; E. Theodore Bachmann, *The Emerging Perspective (Churches and Social Welfare, III)* (N.C.C.C.U.S.A., 1955–56).

movement. Welfare councils too may take stands on public affairs, but in general they tend to be fairly conservative for their main concern is with planning of services and with representing a broad consensus in their approach to the public. However, social workers are often valuable allies—or stimulators—of those who are ethically sensitive, not only because of their knowledge but also because of their general orientation. Many reject complacency. Of course, there have been differences among social workers in this respect, especially in recent years. A growing emphasis on professional competence has tended to diminish the concern for social reform typical of the broad approach of some of the early leaders. Concern with cases or small groups may absorb the individual workers. But some leaders today are calling for a renewed or continuing interest in social action.[6]

In local communities, or neighborhoods of large cities, there are often community councils representative of various voluntary associations such as parent-teacher groups and service clubs as well as churches and social agencies. These have been started with various kinds of leadership, but there has been an expansion in recent years stimulated in some major cities by social workers. Metropolitan welfare councils have sought to increase local participation in social welfare planning. Community councils have often concerned themselves with recreation services because, especially with regard to children, these problems are close to home. Some councils have started as an expression of concern over juvenile delinquency. Councils themselves typically do not operate services, but merely point out a need which some agency may meet. In recent years there has been more attention given to matters

[6] Hillman, *Sociology and Social Work,* pp. 55, 62–63, 68–69; Cora Kasius (ed.), *New Directions in Social Work* (New York: Harper, 1954), pp. xii, 159–60; Benjamin Youngdahl, "Social Workers: Stand Up and Be Counted," *The Compass,* XXVIII (March, 1947), 21–24.

of housing, traffic safety, garbage disposal, and other municipal services which are matters of welfare in a broad sense
but more closely related to city planning, involving local
standards of physical upkeep.

Where health and welfare services are involved, a church
wishing to enlarge its program, or to serve the local community better may be well advised to consult either with the welfare council on a city-wide basis or with the local community
council. In the latter case the consultation should normally
take place with the church as a participant. Any new programs to be undertaken by a church would then commend
themselves because they would clearly not be duplicating another agency's work. A general principle which seems wise for
the church or for a social agency to follow is to ask: Who else
is doing it? Who else can do it? In other words, is this particular program for the aged, or for teen-agers, one which
we are best equipped to do? Is it one which is more closely
related to our main program than to that of some other
agency? There obviously are so many needs in any community
that the church cannot afford to be competitive in its
approach. Its co-operation in planning services will add
strength to whatever is undertaken in the long run.

Urban renewal

In the United States the participation of the federal government in providing for the housing of low-income families got
underway in the 1930's, particularly with the passage of the
United States Housing Act in 1937. The actual construction
and operation of public housing is the responsibility of local
authorities, but they receive aid in the form of loans and
subsidies from the federal government. Public housing
projects were originally intended to replace intolerable and

inferior buildings, but in some places they have been built on vacant land. The emphasis then is on increasing the supply of standard dwelling units available to those people who cannot afford to pay for housing from their limited income.

Federal aid to communities took a new turn with the Housing Act of 1949, which provided not only a continuation of contributions and loans for low-rent housing, but something novel—the possibility of grants for urban redevelopment. The government recognized that some of the blighted areas near the centers of cities had inordinately high land values, forced up by the expectation that the central commercial area would expand to fill them. In order to reclaim these blighted areas, and rebuild them with new housing, the land had to be purchased, then sold again for less than its previous market value. This had been made possible by the federal and local governments working together to encourage private investment and to get back on tax rolls properties that were in many cases tax delinquent.

Federal loans and grants were provided that would absorb up to two-thirds of the loss involved in the purchase and assembly of land later sold or leased to builders for slum clearance. Under this redevelopment program many of the housing projects were built by insurance companies. The federal law required both that provision should be made for the relocation of persons displaced by slum-clearance projects and that any redevelopment plans would have to accord with over-all city plans.

This was a bold new approach which resulted in some major rebuilding in leading cities. An even broader concept was expressed, however, in the 1954 federal legislation when the concept of "urban renewal" was introduced. Communities could, with federal aid, continue public housing and the redevelopment programs, but they were also encouraged to make plans for rehabilitation of borderline areas and for a continuous process of attention to the effects of city growth. Urban renewal includes the idea of conservation, which means that in middle-aged areas a program of slum prevention may be carried out. To maintain the quality of such an area requires attention to municipal housekeeping, to the enforcement of building codes particularly, and possibly to the clearance of eyesores—particular spots which might deteriorate further. Citizen participation is emphasized and local community councils play a new role in relation to conservation.[7]

Special relations of churches to city planning

Rebuilding of areas. A large-scale approach to the redevelopment of some of the core areas of major cities has been made possible by the federal aids which have been described. The construction of public housing projects and large-scale rebuilding by private owners, such as insurance companies, have resulted in the demolition of existing housing sometimes in vast square-mile units. A resulting problem is always the relocation of former occupants of such dwellings. The new buildings may or may not serve the same kind of people. Sometimes there is an influx of middle-income people into areas formerly populated by low-income families.

The existing churches in a rebuilt area also face problems of adjustment. Are their buildings suitable, both functionally and esthetically? Are they prepared to serve the newcomers in their immediate areas, and to help develop a sense of community among people who are strangers to each other? A different kind of problem is presented if the church building itself is marked for demolition. In that case, the church, like

[7] Miles Colean, *Renewing Our Cities* (New York: Twentieth Century Fund, 1953). See also reports of Housing and Home Finance Agency of the U. S. government.

any other property owner, would be paid a fair market value. However, it would doubtless have difficulty finding new quarters, especially if its congregational strength has declined.

Location of churches. Larger questions of policy which affect the merger, relocation, or original location of a church at a particular point will be discussed in later chapters, but certain considerations relate to city planning. Church buildings which accommodate several hundred people or more need to be located on major arteries. In addition, provision should be made for parking. An extra parking lane is useful for the receiving and discharging of passengers, particularly children and older people, and for forming automobile processions. As to off-street parking, there is no magic formula for the number of spaces needed, but careful planning is desirable with due regard to helping maintain the character of the surrounding area.[8] Where land is available, new churches are well advised to procure sites large enough to provide ample parking space, space which might at times during the week be used for playground purposes.

Planners have thought in terms of a superblock, or the neighborhood unit as it is more commonly called, particularly in the rebuilding of parts of a city. The same concept may also be used in new subdivisions or suburban developments. Essentially the neighborhood unit is an area of manageable size, large enough to be somewhat self-contained and to prevent encroachment of pressures from the outside. It is planned so that through automobile traffic is routed along the periphery. Walking is thus made safer within the area. In fact, the walking distance of children to an elementary school is the determining factor in the area of the neighborhood unit.

[8] Fred Bair, Jr., "New Churches and the Law," *The City Church*, VII (January–February, 1956), 2–4. See also comment on this article by Walter Kloetzli in *The City Church*, VII (March–April, 1956), 13.

The school is thought of as the center geographically, and to some extent in social terms as well. Curvilinear streets are generally provided in these newly designed areas, partly for esthetic effect, but largely because traffic is thus reduced and slowed. In general, relatively more area in planned neighborhoods is devoted to playground or open space than to streets, whereas in the conventional gridiron pattern streets may take up 30 per cent or more of the total land area.

Wherever there is a neighborhood unit, or some variation of the basic idea, churches have an obligation to relate themselves to this design in their planning. If a church expects to serve a neighborhood, it should be located near the school at the center of the area. A multineighborhood or regional church accordingly should be located on the periphery in order to make use of the main traffic routes and to provide access from several smaller areas.[9] The location of churches with respect to one another is a matter for local and regional interdenominational concern.

The neighborhood unit is considered a physically healthy cell. Its earlier advocates saw in it possibilities for a new kind of social cohesiveness, greater feelings of neighborliness, to be facilitated by the ease of meeting people and by having one accessible center. Here a neighborhood church might contribute to the building and strengthening of loyalties and co-operative relationships. However, within such a planned local unit there might be people of only one economic group. This or any other form of homogeneity, while it may more easily foster a sense of fellowship, could fall short of the church's ideal of inclusiveness for all sorts and conditions of men. A peripheral church might be less selective. Potentially

[9] Robert C. Hoover and Everett L. Perry, *Church and City Planning* (Survey Guide 2, Bureau of Research and Survey, N.C.C.C.U.S.A., 1955).

it can draw from a wider area and hence attract a variety of people. However, it too may owe its existence to an ethnic loyalty or some other form of social exclusiveness.[10]

Conservation. The role of community councils and the encouragement of citizen participation have been mentioned earlier in this chapter as part of the preventive aspect of urban renewal, which has recently been called conservation. Churches have taken notable parts in conservation areas of many cities. Their concern is twofold: to protect their own properties and to maintain the quality of life in their vicinity.[11] In a way, this is but a new focus for what good citizens have long been doing. Besides what can be done co-operatively in the community, church members who individually care for their houses, shrubs, and back yards, whether they are owners or renters, are thereby contributing to the stability of the area.

Zoning and other regulations. Zoning ordinances vary from city to city, and their interpretation by the courts also varies in different states. One authority has indicated that "in general zoning ordinances do not restrict the location of churches. Those who have drafted many zoning ordinances have taken this for granted and have not mentioned churches in the ordinances, with the result that persons interpreting ordinances later have raised a question as to whether a church can be erected in an area set aside for single-family dwellings. In other situations it was the definite intention to limit church buildings to certain locations."[12] A review of recent court cases casts doubt on the constitutionality of barring churches

---

[10] *Ibid.*, p. 19. See also Arthur Hillman, *Community Organization and Planning* (New York: Macmillan, 1950; Milan: 1953; Rio de Janeiro: 1956), pp. 63–66.

[11] C. J. Curtis, "Changing Englewood," *The City Church*, VIII (January–February, 1957), 12–14.

[12] Wm. Kincaid Newman, "Legal Regulations on Church Building," *Planning 1957*, (Chicago: 1957), p. 22. Report of the San Francisco Conference, May 18, 1957, of the American Society of Planning Officials.

from residential areas. However, the decision in certain cases turned on whether in a given place there was sufficient land available within the limits of the town or municipality for the building of churches and similar institutions.[13]

It appears that California is one of the states where churches have had the greatest difficulty with zoning restrictions. On the other hand, the Florida Supreme Court in 1950 stated: "The church is not bound by some of the regulations imposed on other institutions." A civic official from that state warns, however, "Surely churches should be the last to depend on influence for the protection of special privileges which are demonstrably hostile to the public interest. . . . The new churches, with their daily uses, increased attendance, and wide range of activities, pose much greater problems than the older churches in which use was relatively limited. . . . The time will come when the courts generally will find that there is nothing sacred about noise, congestion, lack of parking facilities and overcrowding of land regardless of the religious nature of the cause of these effects."[14]

A novel approach to zoning, as it affects churches in redevelopment areas, has been suggested by Meryl Ruoss, Executive Director, Department of the Urban Church, Division of Home Missions, N.C.C.C.U.S.A. He has proposed as a zoning concept "useful and neighborhood institutions," suggesting that such a designation might be applied to an area of from two to a half-dozen blocks. In such a zone certain existing churches and neighborhood-serving institutions could remain; to it others might be attracted with some assurance of stability as they make plans to serve the rede-

---

[13] *Ibid.* See also "Land Planning in a Democracy," *Law and Contemporary Problems.* XX (Spring, 1955), 199–350. Cf. Dennis O'Harrow, *Planning Advisory Service* (Information Report 106 of American Society of Planning Officials [Chicago: January, 1958]).

[14] Bair, "New Churches and the Law," *op. cit.,* pp. 2–3.

veloped area. The proposal is receiving favorable consideration in New York City.[15]

Building codes are well known. There may be cities where their unnecessary strictness forces up the cost of new church construction. However, "as to old buildings, the inspectors are often too lenient in dealing with churches. Precautions against fire and other safety measures are for the protection of the churches and their members and should be willingly complied with."[16]

Control of noise is in many cities a growing concern which may have an effect upon the churches. With reference to belfry broadcasts, "electronics has placed small churches on a level with large ones, and some of the small churches have striven to make up in noise what they lack in membership. . . . Noise from churches should receive treatment on the same basis as noise from other sources in the same area."[17]

Ethical issues

Even though planning often has to do with land use and buildings, with material things, the welfare of people is a paramount consideration in the thinking of leading professionals and civic officials. Planning is for people. This is more than a slogan, because coupled with it is the idea of teamwork between planner and citizen. The person whose needs are presumably being served is now more often consulted in the planning process. Also, he can always ask to be heard. In a democracy people ultimately have only themselves to blame if they do not exercise the powers which are basically theirs.

The special interest of churches and of church people in

[15] Meryl H. Ruoss, "The Churches and Urban Redevelopment," *The City Church*, VIII (May–June, 1957), 15.
[16] Newman, "Legal Regulations on Church Building," *loc. cit.*
[17] Bair, "New Churches and the Law," *op. cit.*, p. 4.

planning has been pointed out, but there is also a more general concern which cannot be overemphasized. Dennis O'Harrow, Executive Director of the American Society of Planning Officials, said not long ago, "City planners need badly the support (and constructive criticism) of an 'unselfish' group of people. Most of the pressures that planners are subjected to, and the reason that they frequently bow to inferior development, come from self-seeking persons with a great deal of money to apply pressures where pressures get them what they want. And, in general, I would say that we are more likely to find a consistently unselfish group among church leaders than anywhere else, not excluding the real estate board.

"There are many ethical issues involved in city planning and urban renewal. . . . The church should share in facing some of the problems confronting those who plan and shape the city of tomorrow: Shall families in blighted areas be permitted to 'double-up'—perhaps three families sharing the living space normally required for one? Shall speculative home builders be devoid of responsibility for schools and playgrounds in the mushrooming suburbs—yes, and for provision for church sites? Whose responsibility are the dispossessed—those persons made homeless by redevelopment projects? . . . Shall new or renewed neighborhoods or housing projects be homogenous—or shall they be nonsegregated as to class, age, race?"[18]

The planned rebuilding of slum areas has produced some monumental examples of what can be done to improve housing. So far in major cities only enough has been achieved to demonstrate the possibilities. Reducing population density and improving the quality of housing is part of the broader concern of contemporary planners, as it should be of conscien-

[18] Kloetzli, "Churchmen in Urban Renewal," *op. cit.*, p. 244.

tious churchmen. The experience of overcrowding in shabby, noisy quarters—with dampness, rat infestation, and disproportionately high rents—cannot be readily or sympathetically understood by many Protestant people who are themselves well housed and generally comfortable.[19] The ethical issues inherent in the problem of decent housing standards is one of the supreme challenges to Christian citizenship in the contemporary city.

[19] Galen R. Weaver, "Housing is a Christian Concern," *The Christian Century*, LXXIII (February 15, 1956), 207–09.

5

The Changing Urban Church

As one becomes aware of the many transitions in the American city which are affecting the urban church, it becomes obvious that many new trails still need to be blazed. It is encouraging to note, though, that there have already been some significant pioneering ventures.

Before a congregation can begin to make adaptations and adjustments to its shifting setting, it must first of all evaluate the stereotyped interpretations of its role. Is the congregation attempting to perpetuate a rural-oriented program in the city setting? Is a young married couples' program being promoted because the need exists, or simply because so many suburban churches have one? How much of the program is merely following the stereotype and how much is a response to local needs? With so many factors in the picture, and with the complexity of these factors, it becomes important for thorough community studies to be made. Such studies have helped congregations to evaluate more correctly their own situation as well as the processes of change operative in their neighborhood.

When congregations see themselves realistically in relation to one another and in relation to their communities they can understand more clearly what their planning and programming ought to be. For example, several decades ago perhaps it was necessary for churches to exist in rather close proximity to one another. Today, in many instances, mergers of adjoining churches are called for. Possibly in earlier years there were linguistic or other differences between two congregations, whereas today the make-up of both groups is almost identical. It seems to be a waste of precious funds to maintain two small adjacent congregations where one could serve quite adequately. On the other hand, it is true that in the past city churches have often relocated in an attempt to hold together a constituency rather than to assume new neighborhood responsibilities. Certainly there are times when, after a frank appraisal of its situation, a congregation can, with a clear conscience, decide to relocate.

If an urban congregation really intends to serve as effectively as it possibly can, it must be willing to appraise its situation in all humility and sincerity, considering all of the possibilities, even the possibility of closing its doors. There are numerous cases on record of neighborhoods completely losing their residential character and changing to commercial and industrial areas. Obviously churches are not needed in these places (unless, of course, we are thinking of the downtown church for a denomination).

Not a few congregations these days are asking themselves the question, "How big ought a congregation to be?" There are those who feel that once a congregation numbers more than five hundred adult members there begins to be a change in the relationship between the members. A loss of fellowship or of personal identification with the congregation begins to take place. Certainly when a membership exceeds four or five hundred the congregation has a definite need for a multiple staff.

There are congregations which have faced this matter of size quite realistically. They have started mission churches by deliberately dismissing significant numbers of their membership to start new congregations. As a congregation begins to take quite seriously its responsibility to its immediate neighborhood possibly it will see that it is not the best strategy to allow a single church to become too large. Related to this issue, of course, is the condition and adequacy of the church plant and its ability to house a multistaff program.

Some of the above possibilities may seem radical and dangerous for congregations to consider. However, as we take an over-all view of the metropolitan area, appraising the outreach of Christian congregations into the whole community, we must stand ready to consider fairly all possible courses of action. In a sense this means that the congregation must be willing to lose its life in order to find it. As long as a congregation insists on perpetuating itself or its program merely on the basis of sentiment, tradition, or historic loyalties, new adjustments and adaptations cannot be considered. It is only as a congregation stands ready to surrender to the will of the Lord, and honestly to ask questions concerning its God-given role in the community, that new doors open and solutions appear.

A renewed outreach

Another adjustment of the urban church which is occurring on a nation-wide scale today is the integration of new cultural and racial groups into the membership and life of the congregation. Though only a fraction of the churches that could be embarking on this kind of ministry are doing so, there still are a significant number that are leading the way. As neighborhoods change and older inhabitants of the community are replaced by newcomers of different complexion or cultural background, it becomes imperative that congregations renew their outreach to include all persons. Experience has shown that many of the fears and prejudices of those congregational members who oppose such changes are often unfounded. A new sense of joy and accomplishment often permeates congregations that have "made the break" and launched out into their neighborhoods to welcome people of all backgrounds.

Sometimes the question is asked, "Why shouldn't we let these other people go to their church and we will go to our church? Isn't this really proselyting?" These and a whole host of other rationalizations and defenses can be raised against the integration of a congregation. Our self-studies have actually shown that the percentage of the population that is unchurched is generally higher in the central city or changing neighborhood areas than it is out in the more stabilized and homogeneous suburban areas. This would indicate that in changing neighborhoods missionary and evangelistic opportunities are also greater.

Membership distribution studies of major Protestant groups almost invariably disclose "vacuum areas" in these central neighborhoods.[1] Even where churches are actually situated in such "vacuum areas" substantial segments of their membership are located outside them. It is sometimes stated facetiously that the percentage of a given neighborhood that is "churched" varies directly with the distance of that neighborhood from the city hall.

One of the more significant phenomena in the American church today is the renewed sense of evangelistic outreach. As an understanding of the mobility and changing nature of a neighborhood begins to dawn on city congregations they are launching into evangelism programs with new zeal and fervor. Practically all of the major denominations have now established strong national programs of evangelism with many valuable guides and suggestions for local congregations.

[1] Studies on file at the H. Paul Douglass Library of Religious Research, N.C.C.C.U.S.A., New York.

Systematic work is the order of the day. If interpreted broadly enough evangelism can involve every phase of congregational activity and outreach. For purposes of this discussion, however, evangelism is taken to mean specifically the going out into the community by church members to contact others personally and invite them into the life of the church.

A canvass of the community on a periodic basis is a must. Some congregations have established small committees to maintain a year-round canvassing program, contacting one part of the neighborhood after another. Oftentimes the "Welcome Wagon" and other reception agencies that function so effectively in the middle-class suburbs are nonexistent in the midtown or central city area. This means that the churches lack those sources of additional information which might help them to get acquainted sooner with the newcomer. When one considers the fluidity of the modern urban neighborhood, and the problems of the church in it, it is clear that adequate records and files need to be kept on all contacts that are made. It goes without saying that if people contacted in a neighborhood canvass express their interest in the church, and then are not "followed up," they are likely to feel that the church's corresponding interest in them is not sincere.

Many city congregations have adopted the "shepherding" or "zoning" plan in their evangelism. This is a program whereby the parish area of a congregation, its area of primary responsibility, is divided into fixed subdivisions or zones. In each of these zones one member of the church board or of the evangelism committee is appointed zone captain. It is his responsibility to maintain contact with the church members who are located in that zone and to refer any need for pastoral care directly to the pastor of the church. Likewise he is expected to keep a sort of running check on the people who are moving in and out of the neighborhood in order that the church might quickly and effectively reach out to serve them and to relate them to a church home in their new community. Membership spot maps and other study aids to be described later have proven invaluable in establishing such zoning plans.

As city churches have become more aware of their changing situations they have become more "strategy conscious." Particular efforts have been made to reach out to certain parts of a neighborhood which in the past have not been accessible, into certain types of buildings and also to certain age groups such as young adults. This focusing of evangelism activities has been a conscious development to counter some of the unconscious selectivity of earlier approaches.

Just as there are different types of neighborhoods and classes of people in them so there definitely needs to be different types of evangelism programs. Alienation and isolation are encountered in some of the extremely blighted and deteriorated neighborhoods. People tend to be suspicious of all outsiders and to withdraw in an almost hostile fashion. One church that tried purposefully to open its doors to the newcomers in such a neighborhood found it almost impossible to get them inside the church building. There was a hesitancy, a reticence. In an attempt to overcome this the pastor took the initiative in a new kind of evangelism. He managed to establish contact with one family in a tenement building and was able to arrange for a visit, at which time he discussed with them their family devotions. At his urging, other families from the building were invited into the same apartment on a later occasion. They were allowed to share in the family devotions, and then in a fellowship meal during which many of the barriers began to disappear. This is one example of how the church's evangelism outreach took the initiative to break through into new paths of communication.

In still other neighborhoods where there is a telephone in

every apartment the use of the reverse phone directory was found to be very valuable. This is a directory of telephone users listed by addresses, block by block, rather than in the alphabetical order of their names. When special services or programs are being conducted in the church a committee makes numerous phone calls to residents in the neighborhood, extending to them a personal invitation for the particular occasion.

Personal handwritten or typewritten letters to people in the neighborhood have proven to be another means of evangelistic outreach. People who have had but little contact with the church and who are almost unreachable may sometimes respond to this approach. Such letters can convey to the receiver a personal invitation to worship and fellowship that it might not be possible to extend in any other way. Somehow, new avenues of communication, of breaking through these impersonal barriers of urban life, have to be fostered and developed. These are but a few of the expedients being tried.

As one student of the city church recently stated so succinctly, "We have too many churches in the city that are carrying on a typical rural program, rather than trying to meet the needs of their urban community." One of the more obvious differences between the small-town setting and that of the larger metropolitan center is the degree of isolation or anonymity of the individual. As was pointed out in chapter II, people living near each other just do not know one another. Therefore, word-of-mouth publicity and personal persuasiveness cannot be depended on in the city. The contacts between individuals are too casual and shallow. Actually, as David Reisman so aptly put it, cities are populated by "lonely crowds."[2] Though the contacts of individuals with one an-

[2] Reisman, *The Lonely Crowd.*

other are essential in the communication of the gospel, we need to recognize the importance of publicity and of the printed word, especially in the urban setting. Many churches are finding it very much to their advantage to advertise regularly in local newspapers and to distribute flyers or brochures periodically in their neighborhoods.

In an attempt to further the identification of the isolated member with the congregation and to strengthen the bonds between the members a congregational newsletter or paper has been found very worth while. Some congregations have established a weekly or monthly mailing list of those persons who are actively related to the church, and an occasional mailing list of those persons who are at the very fringe of the life of the church. The more frequent publication is generally of a newsy, house-organ type, whereas the occasional mailing is more on an educational or informational level.

Adjusting present programs

At the heart of the life of the church is the worship service where the Word of God is preached and the sacraments are administered. It is and should be central also to the whole programming and outreach of the church, and must remain central to whatever adjustments may be undertaken for the sake of more effective witness.

Many churches, after having carefully studied their communities and those people whom they would like to reach, have adjusted their schedule of services to make the experience of worship available more often to more people. Some have instituted noonday services for offices and business personnel in the neighborhood. Others have scheduled early services on Sunday morning to reach those who would not otherwise attend the Sunday services. Still other attempts have been made to hold worship services on certain evenings during the week.

Occasionally it may be possible and advisable to consider adjustments in the worship itself. Congregations that have found their neighborhoods radically changed have in some cases altered the make-up of the worship service in an attempt to make it more meaningful for people of a different cultural heritage. Often they include hymns from different backgrounds. In some cases this has meant a departure from the Bach chorale and the introduction of livelier "gospel hymns." Persons from a rural southern background who have never before participated in a formal worship service with large groups of people might feel quite out of place. Perhaps their only previous worship experiences have been in small, closely knit, highly informal groups. A feeling of coldness and strangeness would be very understandable. Certainly the church has a responsibility to be sensitive to the particular needs and backgrounds of all people. Even churches with highly developed liturgical traditions have found within the framework of their worship orders sufficient flexibility to serve this purpose.

In an attempt to help people feel more at home and to become acquainted with one another many churches have instituted a coffee hour either before or after the worship services. In the midst of the anonymity and the loneliness of the big city it is important that the church try to foster a sense of belonging and of community.

Related to the major worship services of the church is the increasing use of the devotional chapel. Many churches see to it that a chapel or room for meditation is available to the public at all times.

Adaptations and expansions in parish education programs promise many new possibilities. Congregations are experimenting with weekday released-time programs as well as evening adult education programs. Generally congregations have found it most effective to run a six- or eight-week institute, one evening a week, with several courses being offered. Possible courses have ranged from such topics as Bible, church history, and basic Christian teachings to discussions of community social problems.

Then, too, there are churches that have instituted special series of noonday lectures for business and working people in the neighborhood of the church. English classes have proven to be of real benefit to many newcomers. Such instruction could include an orientation to community life.

There are churches that have instituted child study groups led by qualified Christian psychiatrists or social workers. Through such groups parents of young children are enabled to relate Christian teachings to the actual everyday problems in their home. In a sense this is a form of counseling, perhaps on a more formalized and academic level. Somewhat on the fringe of the educational emphasis are the day nurseries which several churches have instituted for the children of working mothers.

These are but a few of the possibilities open to churches as they consider the unique problems and opportunities of their neighborhood. Few if any of these different possibilities would have opened up had the churches not first become aware of the need for some new thinking, for re-evaluating their outreach, and for asking if the needed service were otherwise available.

Adjustments in parish administration practices are likewise being made. Many pastors prefer to be free of the bulk of administrative and office chores of the parish. It is understandable, in the face of the increasing demands upon the pastor's busy schedule for counseling, education, and co-ordination, that additional personnel is being secured for urban churches. Parish workers, church secretaries, and business managers become more numerous every day. These are not limited to those churches that can afford such services independently. They are to be found also where churches are banding together to pool resources for the purpose of securing such additional personnel.

Parish records assume greater importance when one considers the constant "turnover" of membership—not to mention the mobility of pastors themselves. Many churches keep complete records of their members. In addition to the usual items they often list the following: occupation, hobbies, participation in organizational life of the church, length of residence at present address, housing status (rental or owner), marital status, and volunteer jobs in the church that might be of interest to the particular person.

Planning conferences for parish life are held every several years, sometimes annually. Generally these are scheduled at a camp or retreat area. Large segments of the congregation spend two or three days together discussing the programming and workings of their congregation. A by-product of such sessions is a new sense of belonging and fellowship among the members themselves.

Greater participation and responsibility in the life of the local congregation on the part of laymen is developing. It is impossible for the contemporary urban church to be a completely "one-man operation." Service is a response to need. Creating awareness of current needs is essential in today's parish administration.

New programs

Many city church pastors say that virtually all of their time could be taken up with the counseling load that constantly confronts them. The strains and tensions of urban life produce an endless stream of troubled people. It seems, too, that the central areas of our cities often attract the disturbed individual. Pastors find it necessary to be extremely selective in their counseling and also to limit the amount of time they devote to any given individual. Several of the larger churches have added specially trained personnel for meeting this tremendous opportunity and responsibility in counseling. Not only have trained pastors been secured for such work, but also clinical psychologists, social workers, and other counselors who have a Christian orientation.

Still other churches have attempted to establish counseling clinics in which some of the people trained in this field make their time available to the church on a limited basis. Certain evenings of the week are set aside for mental health clinics or Christianity and Life sessions, at which a group of professionals work along with the pastor in an attempt to help meet the needs of the disturbed and troubled people in the area.

Likewise, churches which individually lacked sufficient resources have grouped together to hire trained personnel to be available to their several congregations. Such persons might have their headquarters at a welfare society or hospital, or possibly even at one of the churches.

The variety of problems which are brought to the religious counselor are not always "spiritual" or specifically religious. He needs to know his own limitations as a counselor and to have an understanding of his role in relationship to that of the case worker, the psychologist, and the psychiatrist. In many instances the prime contribution of the counselor will be to refer persons for the help they need to another professional.

There are people who for one reason or another do not feel

that they can secure the necessary help from their pastor. Perhaps they do not want to go to the welfare agency either. To meet the need of such persons the downtown church is beginning to develop as a kind of service agency for the rest of the churches in the city. Relative impersonality can be an asset in counseling.

Then too, as they have come to see the importance of the counseling ministry or the pastoral ministry, churches have underwritten the expenses to secure for their own pastor additional training, either part-time or during the summer, in this important field. Many exciting and interesting developments are taking place in this area of ministry to the individual in crisis.

As congregations appraise the make-up of their community and their constituency they are becoming more aware of the senior citizens in their midst—those persons over sixty or sixty-five years of age—for whom boredom and loneliness are often acute problems. They often have much free time and relatively few interests to occupy them. Churches have established leisure time groups, Bible study groups, various craft projects and fellowship circles in an attempt to serve the needs of these retired citizens.

Here again a bridge is established between the congregation and the welfare agencies serving the church. In several urban centers specially trained persons have been hired to help minister to the aged. These persons have gone from congregation to congregation wherever their services were requested, to help groups of volunteers set up programs within the congregation. Not only are these programs established under proper guidance and supervision, but a new understanding of the needs and problems and feelings of this particular age group develops.

Transportation is oftentimes a problem for these people.

Several churches have established transportation pools in order to help their senior citizens commute to the church more easily.

Community concern

The church has long recognized the importance of the family as the basic unit of society. It is in the family that the individual is nurtured in daily growth in grace. It is impossible for the church to be disinterested when it comes to social forces which have an effect upon the well-being of the family. It is understandable, therefore, to find an increasing number of churches concerned about the total community structure, its changes and its problems.

Churches are realizing the importance of adequate housing for normal and wholesome family life. Pastors and laymen in many instances are being actively identified with community conservation programs or urban renewal programs in their cities. Likewise, a new appreciation of the functions of the city planner and his agency is growing (see chapter IV).

When a congregation begins to look upon itself as part of a team, working and serving in a given neighborhood along with other community agencies, new vistas of possibility open up to them. Some churches have feared that to take their place alongside secular social agencies or boards of education or neighborhood conservation groups might somehow minimize the importance and the effectiveness of the gospel. On the contrary, church after church has found that as it is able to discover and relate itself to these various community resources its own hand is strengthened.

In Chicago and Detroit pastors have played major roles in the community conservation program. They and their laymen have actively assisted in the fight against housing code violations and in efforts to improve neighborhood appearances and standards. In Los Angeles churchmen are participating in community councils, helping to integrate and strengthen the agencies serving their community. Some of the precinct captains in New York City make it a point to meet with the clergy of their area periodically to discuss neighborhood problems. These are but a few of the many instances of "teamwork" in the city.

So it is that we find churches more capable of referring people to sources of help, to the family service agency or Alcoholics Anonymous, or perhaps to the board of zoning variances. A host of forces are at work in each urban neighborhood. Churches cannot ignore those forces that are working for the strengthening and the upbuilding of the community.

"It seems safe to say, on the basis of numerous case histories of individual churches, that the parish church is less directly involved in welfare work today than at the time Douglass and Brunner made their study.* Deaconesses who used to visit the poor now have become, instead, directors of religious education. The movement in the 1920's to make city churches community recreation centers, with boys' clubs and bowling alleys and swimming pools, has largely disappeared, and in place of general community programs, churches now tend to have the content of all programs 'church-related,' or oriented specifically to some aspect of church life. Churches have tended to reduce the staff working with welfare needs and increase the staff responsible for education, evangelism, organization, fellowship, and worship."[3]

On the other hand, several urban congregations have added trained social workers to their staffs. These persons have

---

* H. Paul Douglass and E. deS. Brunner, *The Protestant Church as a Social Institution* (New York: Harper, 1935).

[3] Horace Cayton, Setsuko Matsunaga Nishi. Reprinted from *The Changing Scene*, p. 165. Copyright 1955 by the National Council of Churches. Used with permission.

developed programs for groups of various ages and assisted the pastor in his counseling responsibilities. Likewise, they have tried to relate persons in need of help to the agencies in the community able to help them, thus avoiding the wasteful or inefficient practice of providing competing or duplicating services.

A whole new appreciation of group activities in the local congregation has been developing. Through them many of the youth of today are finding ways of relating themselves more wholesomely to one another and to the community at large. Objectives of these group activities include the provision for personal growth in Christian maturity according to individual capacity and need; the adjustment of the individual to other persons, groups, and society; and the motivation toward Christian ideals for himself and for society. Basic Christian teachings and truths become alive and meaningful to these children and youth as they are led to realistic experiences of God's love and of their own dependence upon him.

As a congregation attempts to meet the needs in its community it might well find, as have several churches, that recreation is a pressing problem in the area. In some instances churches have made their plants available to community agencies that were trying to conduct recreational activities for the children and youth of the community. In other cases, congregations have made use of personnel available through local agencies for setting up their own recreational programs. The church ought not to feel that it must have activity of its own in every conceivable area. Rather where there are general needs they ought to be met by the community if at all possible. Perhaps the congregation undertakes recreation responsibilities on a temporary basis until more adequate community facilities are available. Perhaps it becomes an ongoing permanent service.

In some of the extremely blighted neighborhoods of the city there are churches that have established health clinics. They are attempting to bring additional services to those people who are without them. Most of these churches have been able to conduct such programs simply on the basis of using voluntary help. There is one church in an eastern city that has the volunteer services of nine doctors on a part-time basis.

The neighborhood council or community planning council is appearing ever more frequently (see chapter IV). This is an attempt on the part of the various community agencies and institutions to relate themselves to one another and to co-ordinate their activities. Many churches find it extremely worth while to be in on the thinking, planning, and programming of the various health, welfare, and educational agencies in their neighborhood.

Being part of the community team has certain implications for the programming of the congregation and its various auxiliaries. Numerous congregations have brought into their group meetings some of the community leaders of the agencies mentioned above to speak and to discuss with their members the needs of the community, the changes taking place, and the services available or soon to be made available.

In the light of urban studies by the different churches and the recognition by many more churches of the importance of working with community agencies, planning committees have been established within local congregations. The responsibility of this committee is to maintain an ongoing study and appraisal of the community and congregational trends. It attempts to keep before the congregation some of the developing stages of community transition, and what the congregation might be doing in order to serve its community more effectively. Perhaps certain age groups are being neglected. Possibly certain geographical segments of the neighborhood are in need of a particular service. Finally, there might be some matter of social action that ought to be brought before the responsible leaders of the congregation.

6

If We Examine Ourselves

The importance of a realistic appraisal of oneself, or an honest self-evaluation, has been pointed out to us in our Christian teachings. How easy it is for the individual to think of himself "more highly than he ought to think." As fallible persons we are adept at magnifying our virtues and minimizing our faults.

This ability is likewise to be found in groups of individuals —in the life of a congregation, for example. A congregation is likely to be unaware of some of its weaknesses and of the destructive trends which exist. At the same time it is always ready to accept a successful or glowing interpretation of itself. What is needed quite urgently in the midst of these changing urban situations is an honest, humble, and realistic self-appraisal by the congregation.

The importance of congregational self-study

In a Midwest city of some forty-five thousand people three churches joined together in a self-study project. They had for many years considered themselves as mutually complementary; that is, they thought that together they were serving the whole city. To their surprise they discovered when the study was completed that they were collectively serving the same one-third of the city and ignoring the other two-thirds.

Sometimes a lack of assurance may deter some congregations from new programs. There are those that do not know or appreciate their own strengths. Basically this attitude can also be interpreted as a fear of failure. It is reflected in a group's unwillingness to use its creative imagination for fear of not attaining certain standards of perfection.

There seems to have developed a somewhat "standardized" picture of what the average or ideal church should be like. There are churches that have relocated because their leaders wanted to have a "strong Sunday school." However, there are neighborhoods in our American cities where "strong Sunday schools" are not possible, where an effective program designed to serve perhaps the single apartment-dweller or the concentration of retired citizens would be far more necessary. A study of one's congregation and of one's neighborhood as compared to others can help to develop a clearer perception and understanding of the task at hand.

It is entirely possible for some congregations to become so preoccupied in their thinking with the "ideal" or "typical" situation that they are completely blinded to the peculiar God-given challenge and responsibility confronting them in their own location. They experience needless frustration. A further complication is the fact that as population mobility increases in these urban areas many members live a considerable distance from the church, thus making it still more difficult for them to be intelligently aware of their church's neighborhood (see chapters VII and IX).

Actually, the study of one's congregation and community can be a most fruitful experience, shedding new light and understanding on the dynamic situation in which a congregation finds itself. The numerous requests for assistance in such a study indicate a widespread desire for that experience. More and more congregations are asking for a better

understanding of the setting in which they undertake to proclaim Christ as Lord and Savior.

Studies by some five hundred urban churches of the National
Lutheran Council have demonstrated the beneficial effects of
this kind of project. Comments such as these are heard in city
after city: "We just never realized that these things were
happening to our church and to our neighborhood"; "I've
been a member of this church for forty years and certainly
thought that I knew the situation as well as anyone, but believe me, I've learned a great deal from this study"; "If anyone
had told me before this study started that I was going to
learn things and have a different point of view about the
ministry of my church in this neighborhood I would have
been much surprised, but that is exactly what has happened."

As in any venture of this type, there are those who will
express the cynical point of view: "Don't bother me with the
facts; my mind's made up." Then there are those who pride
themselves on their *concrete* thinking—"all mixed up and set"!
Some persons wonder whether it is really the business of the
church to make such studies, studies which seem to them to
be quite secular and unrelated to the work of the church.
Yet some of these very same people become the strongest
supporters of the study as they begin to see unfolding before
their very eyes a detailed analysis of how their congregation
has been succeeding in certain areas and failing in others,
and perhaps of their extreme selectivity in outreach.

In spite of the variety of responses and reactions to a study
program, the need for it obviously exists and it has proven
its worth to countless city churches across the nation from
coast to coast. The average urban congregation is not suf-
ficiently informed about its community and about the changes
taking place within itself. The rapid population expansion
and shifts described in chapter I have made it almost impos-

sible for the casual observer to arrive at a true picture of the fluid urban neighborhood.

When one considers the expansions in city planning and market research expenditures over the last decade, he becomes aware of the importance that business and industry, as well as municipal government, are attaching to this whole matter of objective, scientific community study (see chapter IV). If it is proper or necessary for municipal governments to study carefully the changes in neighborhoods and to map out long-range future planning, it is important that the church likewise be concerned and informed. Business feels it essential that its markets be evaluated—not only those markets which are to be entered in the future, but also those which they are presently serving. (The market is the service area of a particular enterprise.) If it is good for business to be aware of market changes, it is certain that the church needs to be alert to trends in the "service area" of the congregation.

The facts alone do not speak for themselves. Sometimes the assembled facts are so clear, distinct, relevant, and acceptable to a group of persons that they do tell a very significant story. It has been the experience in many studies, however, that this is not always the case. In the first place, facts can be distorted to fit a preconceived idea of what they ought to say. Secondly, they can be selected by choosing some and ignoring others in order to substantiate a particular point of view. Thirdly, they can be compartmentalized in our thinking so that they are not particularly relevant to any course of action by the congregation. This points to the need, not only for a gathering of facts, but for an adequate interpretation and assimilation of these facts.

An example can serve to illustrate this. An analysis of per capita income distribution by neighborhoods or by census tracts indicates that a church is located in a low-income area, that the income of the people has been dropping and will probably continue to drop. One conclusion might, therefore, be that the church ought to move to a higher income area. Another conclusion (perhaps a more Christian one) might suggest that because of the low income there are special problems faced by the neighborhood residents and that perhaps the church in such an area has a special kind of opportunity and responsibility. The first point of view focuses solely on the welfare of the institution, the church. The second point of view gives primary consideration to the area needs and to the service the church might render. Facts can mean different things to different people!

Facts can also mean different things at different times. Timing in a study is of real significance. For a group of churches to work together through a community study should require approximately five or six months. (See the Appendix, pages 170–172, for a "Suggested Timetable for a Congregational and District Self-Study.") Sufficient time must be allowed for the congregations to discuss the information at their various auxiliary and board meetings, and for the information to be assimilated into or integrated with the ongoing thinking and planning of the congregation. The actual work of preparing the congregational maps and charts is really only a matter of perhaps a week's effort. (See Appendix page 165 for a concise listing of these "Recommended Study Aids.") However, if this data is to have significance for the thinking and programming of a congregation there must be ample time for "digestion" of the data.

Community resources

There are numerous community resources which can be extremely helpful in such a venture. As mentioned previously, the city planner and the urban renewal agency have valuable information. They can tell how the land is presently being used, what changes in land use currently loom on the horizon, and what the long-term trends are. Then too, the various kinds of urban renewal programs described in chapter IV will have a bearing on the church's future in a neighborhood. Leaders from these agencies are ready and able to speak to church groups to help them better understand their communities.

The council of social agencies, or welfare council, has information on the neighborhood characteristics of a metropolitan area. They have generally translated Census Bureau data into map form for the use of citizen groups. Again, speakers from these agencies are capable of further interpreting the population, housing, and neighborhood characteristics as described in the maps.

There is an ever growing number of people and agencies whose jobs call for community study and planning of some sort. It is not necessary that all sources be contacted. Also, it should be noted that specific titles and functions vary from city to city. Listed below are some of the "specialists":

City planner
City engineer
Utilities research
Board of education
Recreation commission
Juvenile and domestic relations court
City or county courts
Regional planner
U. S. Department of Labor
Welfare research

Chamber of commerce
Sociology professors
Health department
Highway engineer
Slum clearance commission
Real estate leaders
Council of churches
U. S. Census Bureau
Zoning authorities
Market analysts
Urban renewal agency

Community information

From these and other sources it should be possible to compile maps, tables, and charts showing some or all of the following information according to census tracts:

Land use
Land annexation
Population density
Change in population density
Income distribution
House valuation
Median rental
New housing—in the past decade, the past year, and the next year (estimated)
Highways—existing and proposed
Schools—existing and proposed
Water and sewerage—existing and proposed
Population
Negro-white distribution
Spanish-speaking or other minority distribution
Redevelopment or slum clearance maps

The congregational self-study organization

A committee of approximately six to eight persons should be appointed by the pastor and the official board to plan and conduct the congregation's self-study program. This committee should be as representative as possible. There should be near-by members as well as distant members, new members and senior members, those who have been active in the leadership of the church as well as those who have been on the fringe. Some of the various auxiliaries should be represented.

It is suggested that the committee not be restricted in any way but rather that it be an inclusive and representative group.

A chairman and secretary should be appointed. The pastor should be an ex-officio member of the committee. It should be the duty of the chairman to see that the necessary study assignments are carried out as suggested, and that meeting dates and programs are cleared and properly scheduled.

The importance of area-wide co-operation

The complexity and the anonymity of city life make it quite difficult for congregations to feel a sense of kinship with one another or to experience the bonds of Christian fellowship which we so often talk about. We frequently repeat that we are "one body in Christ," that we are "members of the household of faith." Yet the tendency is for each congregation to go its own separate way, being related to other congregations very often only through the synodical or jurisdictional structure.

More can be gained in this study process if several churches will undertake the project together. That would provide an opportunity to compare data from the various neighborhoods and various types of congregational situations. Many times, as a by-product of such an experience, some of the barriers between congregations have begun to disappear.

The study programs conducted by the National Lutheran Council have attempted insofar as possible to deal with metropolitan areas in their entirety. This decision was based on the fact that even though neighborhoods and areas within larger cities are so cut off from one another, yet as one analyzes processes of change in a metropolitan area it becomes apparent that areas are also closely interrelated. When population shifts, people move from one neighborhood to another. It is interesting to note that the federal government, before it will grant assistance for a specific localized urban renewal project, insists that there be a comprehensive master plan of the entire metropolitan area, not just a study of the neighborhood involved. It further requires that there be comprehensive zoning and enforcement of the zoning regulations (see chapter IV). This should indicate to the churches that it is important to appreciate the combined witness of the total church in the total community. No single neighborhood can really be understood or appreciated apart from its setting in the whole urban scene. This is why congregations need to work together in any study project.

Area organization

A central or intercongregational study committee should be established. This committee may be made up of the chairmen of the study committees of the participating congregations, together with the pastors of the churches. At the initial meeting of this committee a general chairman and secretary should be elected by the group. It is recommended that this committee assume the responsibility for handling the finances of the study project and for determining the over-all timetable and scheduling. This group should secure the necessary resource speakers for the series of meetings held during the course of the study. Likewise, they should make whatever arrangements are necessary for the final workshop or retreat which climaxes the study project. (See the Appendix, pages 172–174, for a "Suggested Agenda for a Final Workshop.")

Whatever area is decided upon by the committee for the boundaries of the study, it would be advisable for all sister churches in that area to participate. As will be explained in chapter VII, the composite maps constructed on the basis of individual congregational maps tell quite a story. If one or several congregations are missing from this composite picture obviously gaps in the information they disclose will become apparent.

In an undertaking of this sort financial responsibilities are inevitably involved. Approximately fifteen to twenty cents per active member has generally been found adequate to cover the study expenses in most urban areas. The contribution of each congregation should be given as early as possible to the secretary of the central committee. It is usually his task to handle the funds, secure the necessary materials and pay the related bills. Included in the costs of the study are such things as maps, translucent paper, mailing, mimeographing, resource speakers, films, and travel expenses. Whatever unused funds remain after the completion of the study are generally re-funded to the participating congregations.

Group discussions

For most of the participants in the study process this will be the first venture of its kind. With such pioneering experiences come certain feelings of doubt, inadequacy, and inferiority. The chairman of the study committee ought to assume as his responsibility the fostering of participation by as many people as possible and expression of whatever ideas they care to submit. There are no pat answers or set formulas for the solving of problems raised by the study. Actually, the person who feels that he has a lot of ready answers to the situation perhaps has not really given due consideration to many of the new study findings as they come along.

The seating arrangement can be helpful or detrimental to discussion. If the group is comfortably seated around a table or several tables, and if the meeting is conducted in a rather informal way, it tends to be more conducive to the expression of opinions and attitudes by all concerned. On the contrary, if the session is conducted on a purely lecture-type or formal basis there will be considerably fewer participants in the discussion.

At the larger district meetings (those attended by all participating churches together) there will doubtless need to be portions of the meeting conducted in formal lecture style—especially when specially invited resource speakers are addressing the assembled group. Even here, however, there should be ample time for discussion following the presentation. It is suggested that perhaps one-third to one-half of the resource person's time be spent in a question-and-answer period. (See the Appendix, pages 174–175, for "Suggestions for Fostering Discussion in the Study Process.")

Following the major presentation and the general business of the larger district meetings, it is advisable for congregational groups to assemble by themselves to discuss further some of the findings and facts. Toward the end of the meeting, opportunity should be given for the separate congregational groups to report back to the general assembly.

Experience has shown that "coffee and cake" during district and congregational study meetings is an excellent way in which to bring together persons of various backgrounds and congregational connections.

The success and effectiveness of the study will depend not so much on the facts themselves, but rather on the impact these facts have upon the thinking and the lives of the members of the participating congregational committees. Therefore it is important that there be honest discussion and sincere searching for answers and for understanding. There is need for special grace to overcome stereotyped habits of thought

about the local congregation and its history, about the surrounding area, and the people now actually living there. As
the children of God prayerfully seek the guidance of the Holy
Spirit and become obedient to his will, they can become more
effective witnesses for Christ.

7

Mapping the Church and the Community

Before a self-study committee of the congregation (or of several neighboring congregations) can begin to interpret what has been happening in its neighborhood, and certainly well before it can begin to make its recommendations toward more effective action and outreach of the church in the community, it will need to know the facts. It will want to know in detail what the trends have been in church membership, in Sunday school enrolment and participation, in the organizational life of the congregation, and in the recent financial picture of the church. It will seek to know what the outreach of the church has been in the community and the results of any recent evangelism and stewardship projects. It will want to know the distribution and spread of the congregational membership and of the Sunday school—where and how far from the church the members live. It will want to know the facts as to how the church has met the needs not only of its present membership but also of the community in which it is located. For this it will need to know the facts about its community or neighborhood.

As it gathers these facts together, the committee will be gaining new insights into the life of its church and of its neighborhood. Offhand impressions and casual observations will be challenged, changed, or verified. Visually presented, the facts unearthed by the committee will often tell a most dramatic story—a story of changes and trends of which neither it nor the church itself has been aware.

Fortunately for the committee there have been developed a variety of tools for gathering together the various facts of the life of the church in its community, as well as skilful techniques for presenting these facts in a graphic form most helpful to their interpretation and understanding. (See the Appendix, page 165, for a complete listing of "Recommended Study Aids.") Among these tools and techniques the committee will find that one of the more helpful in the initial stages of its project is the community map on which is spotted the membership distribution of the congregation.

The membership distribution map

For the city church a map of the specific neighborhood in which it is located is not always the true map of the membership extension of the church. At one time, the members of the congregation may all have lived within the range of several blocks of the church, but for many Protestant city churches that day is past. For this reason, a map showing the distribution of membership, the current picture of one aspect of the church's outreach, is an essential part of the study of the church in its community. It should be one of the first major undertakings in the fact-finding work of the self-study committee. From the addresses of the communicant members the committee may get a general idea of the extensiveness of the geographic spread, but the true picture of emerging patterns within this spread can best be seen through the use of the spot map on which the location of each member is marked with a small ink dot at the place of his residence. If the spread of the congregation is not too extensive the committee might use a map of the church's community or neighborhood on which to plot its membership. If the membership spread is quite extensive, as is the case of most urban churches today, a map of a wider area should be used, one that is large enough in scale and size to show membership patterns clearly.

With the completion of the membership distribution map, insights and questions will already be in the making. Noting the location of the church in relationship to its members spotted on the map, the committee should be able to have a vivid picture of the direction in which the church is reaching out into the city. Many churches are reaching out beyond their location, following the movement of their members outward rather than reaching in toward the central area of the city. Other churches may be reaching out in several directions. With others, outreach may be concentrated in a single area of the city or in those areas easily accessible to main routes of traffic or public transit.

One of the more important uses of the map will be that of determining the general boundaries of the area served by the church. These boundaries can be designated as those within which the largest proportion of the membership is concentrated, with due allowance being made for natural and man-made boundaries between various sections of the city, such as hills, waterways, industrial areas, and major traffic arteries. Some churches, like the downtown church, may have so extensive a scattering of membership that its boundaries are coextensive with those of the city itself, or even of the whole metropolitan area. Other churches may have a broad scattering, yet within a certain section of the city. Still others are likely to have a great concentration within a small area of the city but not necessarily in the immediate vicinity of the church.

The committee will want to know how many, and what proportion, of the total membership live within the immediate community of the church, or within a radius of one to two miles of the church location. It will also want to know if within this more immediate community of the church there are not gaps in the membership distribution—areas into which the church is not now reaching. There will be no end to the questions asked and to the insights gained as the committee studies its membership distribution map.

Other distribution maps

One of the questions the self-study committee may be asking as it examines its membership map is that concerning the extent to which the church is reaching out to its immediate neighborhood. The same question will be raised again as the committee turns to its next undertaking, that of a spot map showing the spread of Sunday school enrolment. This map can be prepared by using a translucent overlay placed over the membership map and plotting, again with an ink dot, the address of each active Sunday school member 14 years of age or under. (Engineering tracing paper such as Bruning 350 T serves well as a translucent overlay.)

Many questions will come to mind with this as with the former map. Perhaps the Sunday school map will show that the children of the school come essentially from the homes of church members, with a distribution just as scattered. Or the map might show that through the Sunday school the church is reaching the immediate community alone, that the children of the more distant members are attending elsewhere or not at all. With the Sunday school map the committee will want to note carefully the role played by such barriers within the community as streets with heavy traffic, industrial sections, and commercial districts. In some cases, the Sunday school is limited to those children who live within walking distance but not beyond main routes of traffic. The fact that in some Sunday schools there are many members from a single block and few or none from an adjacent block might raise questions for the committee, as might the picture of a Sunday school membership concentrated in only one section of the immediate neighborhood of the church.

Just as a Sunday school distribution map is helpful to the committee when seen in relation to a membership distribution map, so too is a map showing the distribution of the various leaders within the church and its organizations, including Sunday school teachers, auxiliary officers, and board members. Again, as with the Sunday school members, each leader is spotted at his place of residence by a single ink dot on another translucent overlay. In many communities of the city the first residents to move outward from the old neighborhood are often those persons most apt to serve in leadership capacities—in political organizations, community centers and councils, scout organizations, local service clubs, and church organizations. As the committee looks at its third map, the leadership distribution map, it will be asking whether or not "absentee leadership," as it has sometimes been called, is a factor in the leadership of the church. Very often a self-study committee will find this to be the case. Its leaders may be living in some of the more distant areas of the congregational spread rather than in the immediate vicinity of the church. Some churches, however, will find that their leaders are evenly distributed across the spread of membership distribution in the city. A few churches might even find that leadership is concentrated in the vicinity of the church, while membership is scattered.

A fourth map—a spot map showing the residence of new

members received in the last ten years—can be a fruitful map in that it describes graphically the growing edge of the church. Here, too, comparisons with the several other spot maps completed will be helpful. The map showing location of new members may disclose that there are areas within the congregational spread where there are only new members but no old members. Or it may show, when compared to the membership map, that there are areas with many old members but no new members. The map of new members may portray vividly that the evangelistic outreach of the church has been uniform throughout the entire area of the wider church boundaries. Or it may reveal that the church's outreach is primarily within its immediate vicinity. Comparison with the Sunday school map can raise many questions, particularly when the two maps are seen in relation to the membership map. It may be that Sunday school enrolment is concentrated in the same areas as the new membership of the church, not in those areas where there are predominantly only older members. The leadership map, studied in relationship to the map showing residences of new members, may show that neither the new members nor their areas of residence are represented in the leadership of the church.

The use of spot distribution maps

These four spot distribution maps, the membership distribution map, the Sunday school map, the leadership map, and the map of new members received in the last ten years, are the basic mapping tools for the self-study committee's understanding of the outreach of the church in the community. But they must be seen in their proper perspective, in terms of the processes of city life which they reflect. They are not pictures of a static pattern of church membership distribution. Rather they should be seen in the context of the changing patterns of the city itself within which the church is functioning. For this reason, the construction of these basic maps at periodic intervals can help the church to see the trends operative within its own outreach in the city, as these are influenced by the changing city itself.

While these four distribution maps are the basic tools for a self-study of the church, the spot map technique may be used for the study of many aspects of the church. Should the church have a parish school or Christian day school it would be essential that the enrolees of this school be spotted on a similar map and then compared with the other four distribution maps. The spotting of a vacation Bible school might be instructive, especially when it is compared with the Sunday school enrolment picture. Other helpful maps might be one spotting Sunday school members coming from homes of non-members, or one spotting active members according to the regularity of their attendance, or according to the amount of their contributions.

Where several congregations are conducting a self-study jointly, it is helpful to bring together the results of their membership distribution maps and to plot a joint picture on a composite map, showing their collective outreach in the same area of the city. If, for example, the churches of a certain denomination in a particular area of the city are conducting a joint study, a composite map, made by combining the maps of each congregation, will provide a good picture of the membership distribution of that denomination across the area.

For census purposes most cities of the United States have been divided into many small areas on the basis of population and population characteristics as well as of natural or physical boundaries. These census tracts, each of which usually comprises between three and six thousand population, are help-

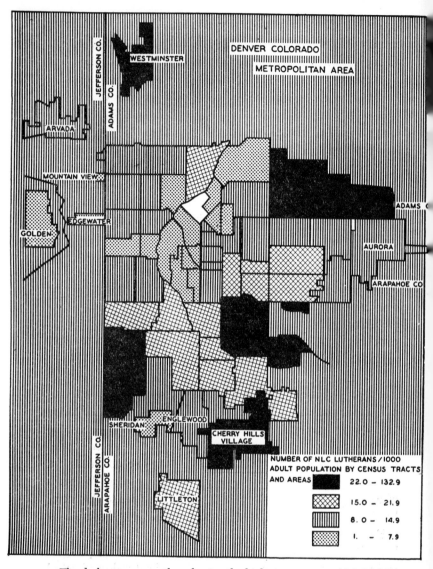

The darkest areas are those having the highest percentage (2.2–13.3%) of Lutheran members in their population. The next darkest areas have a slightly lower Lutheran percentage. Note the extremely low coverage in the central area of the city. The statistics represent only those Lutherans whose churches are affiliated with the National Lutheran Council.

ful in the construction of composite maps. Rather than
spotting the membership of the co-operating churches on a
single map, a count of members by census tracts can be made
in a joint study. Then by comparing the churches' combined
membership with the total population of the census tract a
fair picture of the intensity of denominational outreach in a
particular area of the city can be determined.

Composite maps of membership distribution, Sunday school
distribution, leadership distribution, and new-member distribution can be compared with one another as were the
corresponding spot maps of the individual congregations.
Here again, quite a number of unusual features might be seen
by the joint self-study committee. The leadership of the
several churches, for example, might all be concentrated in a
single area of the city, a single census tract. Or the Sunday
school membership of all of the churches might likewise be
concentrated in a single area—perhaps in a tract at the center
of the studied churches. (See the Appendix, pages 166–168, for
"Steps in the Construction of Composite Maps.")

Further map resources

The spot distribution maps and the composite maps should
always be understood in terms of the communities in which
the church members live. From its spot maps a church is able
to learn much about itself, the extensiveness of its outreach,
its gaps and its areas of strength, and also the boundaries or
limits of its outreach. It should then be able to look at the
facts about its neighborhood and surrounding communities to
see how its own outreach has possibly been affected by
changes or trends within the city itself.

The self-study committee will find as it progresses with its
work that there are a wealth of community resources near by

which are ready and willing to offer continuing aid in many aspects of the project. Helpful to the committee and to the church as it looks at its own distribution maps and as it seeks to understand its relationship to the community, would be a number of further map resources obtained from, or shared in consultation with, the various planning, housing, zoning, and welfare agencies of the city. Among such helpful aids would be the maps of local and city planning commissions on which are located the different kinds of land uses in the community—residential, commercial, industrial, and others; or the zoning maps issued by city officials on which are designated the various building-type zones of the community —for single-family homes, apartment houses, commercial districts or industrial establishments. Also of help might be the city or local housing and redevelopment authorities and agencies and their information regarding current and projected physical changes in the community such as housing developments or land clearance. From local departments of public works or from local recreation and park departments information can be secured regarding the construction of expressways and through ways, parks and playgrounds, and other public works. Many of these community resources have prepared their information in a dramatic visual map form, and the committee will do well to examine it closely.

With the help of such aids as are available to them, the committee will look at the actual physical layout of the community in which its church is located or the membership concentrated. Here the church will see itself in relation to its own setting—in relation to the shopping centers and commercial areas of the community, the industries and railways, parks, schools, community centers, and other local institutions, including the other churches. In itself, such a picture may not seem important. Viewed, however, as a picture of the living, changing city which the church has entered in order to accomplish its task, the map of the physical layout of the neighborhood takes on new life.

From its distribution maps the church is able to point out those areas within the neighborhood and the surrounding communities in which it has strength of outreach, as well as those areas in which such strength is lacking. A look at the physical layout of the community and at the relation of the church's outreach to this same layout often gives a self-study committee a quite different picture from what it had imagined, even though they be residents of that very community. For example, they may realize for the first time that industrial expansion near the church is actually cutting it off from a considerable segment of the community, or that a planned expressway or housing development is certain to change the immediate physical setting of the church and its accessibility. For the first time committee members might realize the actual distance between the various churches of the community. For example, they may discover a single church located all by itself in one section of the community, while in another section a number of churches are located all within walking distance of one another. Even the patterns of streets or of traffic and public transit and their relation to the outreach of the church and to its effectiveness might be visualized with new insight as the church looks at the physical features of its local area.

The maps and materials of city and local planning commissions would be of special importance to the study committee. From them the church might find any number of community features relevant to its own planning and to an understanding of its program. The proximity of industry, of commercial districts or of railways should be noted. Questions might be raised regarding their effect upon the church in the community. The nature and condition of housing should also

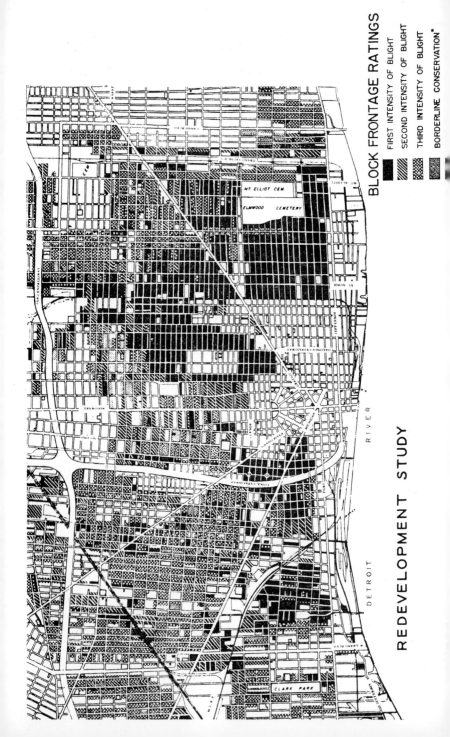

REDEVELOPMENT STUDY

BLOCK FRONTAGE RATINGS

▮ FIRST INTENSITY OF BLIGHT

▨ SECOND INTENSITY OF BLIGHT

▧ THIRD INTENSITY OF BLIGHT

▨ BORDERLINE CONSERVATION*

be noted. Here the questions raised may even lead to recommendations that the church become active in matters of housing and neighborhood conservation and redevelopment. Zoning maps and the materials of redevelopment authorities and of public works departments should be studied carefully to discover trends and developments which might well influence the future of the church. Perhaps the community of the church has recently been rezoned to allow new kinds of land uses and building structures in the neighborhood, many of which would drastically change the neighborhood scene and the work of churches within it. Certainly the committee will need to pay careful attention to planned and projected future physical changes in the community. More than one church has suddenly awakened to the fact that an expressway or superhighway was cutting across its front yard, even though the highway itself had been in the planning stage for a number of years. Each of these resources, and many more of the committee's own finding, will be helpful to the church as it endeavors to see itself within a community perspective. Their information can often be enlightening to church members as they plan their strategy of future outreach and seek to fulfil their community responsibilities within the neighborhood.

Census materials

If the self-study committee has given attention to census tracts in its construction of spot distribution maps and composite maps, it will be able to use the published census

Cities are making comprehensive studies of their needs for rebuilding or conserving older neighborhoods. In this careful study of the Detroit central city area, the darkest blocks are those requiring most urgent attention. The next darkest group of blocks require secondary attention. Those blocks that are unmarked require merely the conservation of their present condition.

materials relating to these tracts in its investigation of the population characteristics and trends within the area. It may ask, "What are the characteristics of those areas of the city where membership is concentrated as over against those areas where it is not?" If there is a marked absence of members from the immediate area of the church and a concentration of members at some outlying area, census tract materials may provide the clues to the underlying reasons in case they are not already known to the committee. Many facts about the life of the community hitherto completely unknown may be unearthed. For example, the committee may find that, while its own congregational membership is made up mainly of families and not of single people, the immediate neighborhood shows a concentration of single people who are perhaps not being reached by any church. Or it may find, contrary to its own impressions, that an extremely high proportion of the mothers of the neighborhood are working during the day. This could possibly mean adjustments in the hours for church auxiliary meetings, or new departures in the field of day care for children.

Census materials are available on a small-area or census tract basis for many of the larger cities. A self-study committee, in examining them, would be most interested in such listed characteristics as the racial and national background of the tract population, the number of school years completed by persons over twenty-five, the median family income, and the number of persons who have moved into the area during the census year—a clue to the mobility trends of the community. It would also be interested in seeing what the age breakdown is in the various areas of its concern, as well as the number of single persons compared to the number of married, and the employment status and occupational groups represented in the area.

The committee, however, should be selective in its use of census materials as in its use of the other resources available to them. Too often a single fact can be exaggerated into a "trend" far beyond what it really is. For this reason the committee should always be willing to call upon the many resource persons of the wider community who will be able to interpret these facts clearly and in proper proportion. Schools and community centers can provide information concerning changes in the population since the last census year. Welfare agencies and councils can be helpful in pointing out changes in the health and social welfare needs of the community. Often these same agencies have more recent information relating to the present characteristics of the neighborhood than is available in publications of the Bureau of the Census.

A strategy for the future

Through use of the assortment of maps available to a self-study committee, through such mapping techniques as the spot map or the composite map, and through the careful examination of these same materials in the light of a city perspective, the picture of the outreach of the church into its community becomes clarified. Possibly the church will see that its congregation, as a body, has drifted outward from the old neighborhood surrounding the church, and that the incoming population has not even been touched by the outreach of the church or its members. The church may discover facts which disclose an extremely disjointed church life, inconsistent outreach and scattered effectiveness. On the other hand, it may discover the real strengths of its work— strengths never realized before. As the study committee analyzes these materials it will be working toward future recommendations —toward a strategy for the future.

From the use of just a few maps of its own making the committee may move out into completely new areas of concern. Running through its recommendations, as the church proceeds to plan its future, should be at least an ongoing awareness of the changing physical features of the community: deteriorating housing conditions or expressways being built through the center of the neighborhood; an awareness of the changing human features of the community: new groups moving into the area and their special needs, old residents drifting away sometimes to a great distance from the church; and an awareness of the church's obligation to serve the community. Continual attention should be given to these changing features of the neighborhood, both human and physical, for they are strong determinants of the future outreach of the church. Community characteristics, physical changes, trends in health and welfare needs, and forecasts of the community picture of the future are constantly being mapped and remapped by planning and redevelopment authorities, welfare agencies and councils, and civic officials. The self-study committee should make intelligent use of these materials in preparing their strategy for the future.

8

Charting the Congregation

Essential as they are, the spot distribution maps constructed by the self-study committee tell but a portion of the story of the church in its community. Even the additional maps and materials illustrating the changing physical features and human characteristics of the community do not complete the picture. The fact-finding work of the committee must move on into the second portion of its study, the charting of the congregation.

Again, numerous tools and techniques which have proven most helpful to congregational self-study groups may be utilized. (See the Appendix, page 165, for a complete listing of the "Recommended Study Aids.") Like the mapping techniques, these tools for the charting of the congregational picture are also aids toward a visual portrayal and graphic presentation of the life of the city church. Just as the maps portrayed, often in dramatic form, aspects of the church of which the committee members may have been only casually aware, so too will the congregational charts bring into new perspective much of what has been happening within the church. The use of translucent paper for these study aids is suggested.

Line graphs on membership and finance

An often stimulating beginning to the charting of the congregation can be made by charting the membership trends of its recent history. A single line plotted across a graph can be used to recount the rises and drops of membership through the years. From church records, or from church or synodical annual reports, the communicant membership of the church for each year can be obtained. It should be charted on the graph, by year and by number of members. Churches have found that historical perspective is most important in such a chart. If possible begin with a date of at least thirty years prior to the year of the study. Younger churches should begin with the year of origin, perhaps even dividing the scale of years across the base of the chart into four- or six-month periods. Committee members may have been aware of some of the fluctuations in church membership during recent years. Yet until they view these same annual changes on such a chart they are not able to catch the longer perspective of years or discern the possible emerging trends. Comparison of this chart with the membership distribution map and with the map showing the distribution of new members is very likely to provide an interesting picture of developments in membership trends in the church.

A chart of Sunday school enrolment over the same period of time will serve a similar useful purpose, especially as it is studied in relation to the other study materials such as the Sunday school distribution map. It should be constructed like the church membership chart, using the same vertical scale of numerical count and the same horizontal scale of years. Charting the cradle roll membership on the same graph with a dotted or colored line will be an additional aid to the study committee, particularly in its analysis of the participation of younger families in the life of the church.

Another line graph, to be drawn in like manner and to the same scale as the graphs of congregational and Sunday school memberships, is the chart of financial trends during the same

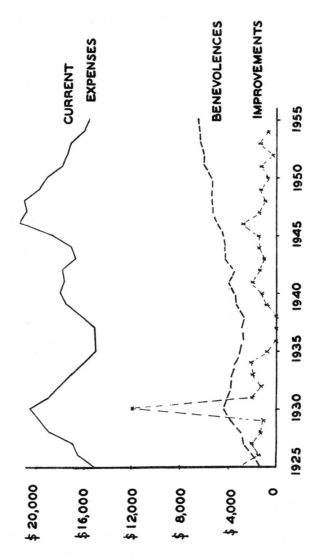

A graphical analysis of the financial picture of the congregation can prove very helpful. The total expenditure in any given year can be computed by adding the three subtotals (example: in 1954, improvements equal $500; benevolences equal $6,000; current expenses equal $15,000; total equals $21,500).

period of time. The committee may wish to construct three distinct lines across this graph of congregational giving: a line portraying current expenses; another showing giving to church benevolences; and a third indicating funds for capital improvements, such as a new church building. The committee will want to compare this chart with the membership chart, noting whether or not the fluctuations in financial trends correspond to fluctuations in membership trends, or if there have been other discernible patterns in the finances of the church.

The three line graphs, membership, Sunday school enrolment, and financial trends, are commonly used techniques for the understanding of congregational trends. Obviously they are not in and of themselves gauges of church effectiveness. Neither a steadily rising line across the membership chart nor a steady growth in giving are necessarily signs of effective labor in the city "vineyard," just as a steadily declining membership is not necessarily a certain sign that the church is failing in its task. These several techniques measure trends, it is true, yet trends that must always be seen within the context of all that has constituted the sources of these trends, both in the church and in the city.

The composition of the congregation

As a church studies its trends in membership growth or decline it may become aware of the fact that there have been important shifts within the composition of its membership. Changes in the congregational make-up, in fact, may have determined the fluctuations in numerical membership through the years. They may even have influenced the geographic patterns of membership location revealed in the spot distribution maps. Offhand impressions may be prevalent that the congregation is composed mainly of family units rather than of single persons. The membership may popularly suppose that they are primarily of German heritage, or Swedish or Negro, and that this has been the case for a number of years. Likewise, a church may have the idea that with respect to age there is an even spread through the congregation; or that, as in many churches, there are probably more women than men, though not to the degree of overbalancing the picture; and that this too has been the case for generations.

A self-study committee will want to examine carefully the make-up of its congregation in order that it might understand how the facts of its congregational composition relates to the recent trends of membership in numbers and in distribution, to the present outreach of the church and to its future work. Particularly helpful in comparing the make-up of the congregation with that of the community in general is an age and sex breakdown of the membership as it can be portrayed through the population pyramid.

The population pyramid

The population pyramid is a graphic technique for portraying and analyzing the age and sex composition of a particular group of people. Essentially, the pyramid is a series of horizontal bars, each representing a particular age group, and each extending to the right and to the left of a center vertical line. That portion of the bar extending to the right of the center represents, as a percentage of total population, the female persons in that particular age group. To the left of center the bar represents the male persons of the same age group.

Such a population pyramid can illustrate well the age and sex composition of a congregation. It is especially useful for purposes of comparison with the corresponding patterns of age and sex distribution for the community in general. A comparative study of population pyramids of the various areas of the city, for example, will show many contrasts and variations between the older, long-stabilized community, the younger neighborhood, and the inner city area composed mainly of recent in-migrants from rural areas. The older community will have a much smaller proportion of young children and of persons under thirty-five than does the younger neighborhood or the in-migrant area (see chapter I, p. 9). Comparison of a congregation's pyramid with that of the community in which the church is located, or in which the members live, may show as interesting a contrast.

The committee can assemble the data for an age-sex pyramid of the congregation by first making a tally of the total church membership according to age and sex groups, including Sunday school, day school (if any), and cradle roll membership; totaling this tally for each division separately, then translating each of the several divisional totals into a respective percentage of the grand total membership count. With the completion of the membership pyramid the committee will want to compare their findings with the pyramid of the community or neighborhood. This can be done by turning again to their census tract materials in which population is enumerated by age and sex, or, if this material is outdated, to the most recent estimates of the population composition of the area. Certainly, such an area should include the neighborhood of the church, even though membership is not concentrated there. Perhaps the community age-sex pyramid shows a high proportion of persons over the age of sixty while the congregational pyramid shows an extremely low proportion in that category. Or maybe the opposite is the case. Compared with the city as a whole, the church's community might have a high percentage of young people while the church is strongest in the age brackets over fifty. If this is the case, the church might have noticed the effects already in the trends in its own membership or in the Sunday school.

For purposes of comparison it will be essential for the study committee to construct all pyramids in similar manner and to similar scale. Pyramids of the leadership and of the new members received in the last ten years who are still active may prove even more instructive than the pyramid of membership at large. Again, these pyramids should be interpreted in the light of the other study findings, especially the findings relative to the neighborhood picture. For example, the committee will want to examine the new-membership pyramid to see whether the persons brought into the church conform more or less to the general age-sex distribution of the community, or whether the church instead is attracting persons of one particular age or sex group and not those of another. If the general church membership pyramid shows a lower proportion of persons over sixty than does the community pyramid, the committee will want to study the new-membership pyramid to see if there have been any gains at all in reaching the older residents of the neighborhood. If the congregational pyramid shows a lower percentage of younger people than the community pyramid the new-membership picture may shed light on the effectiveness of the church's current outreach to young families and youth in the area. Looking at the leadership pyramid, the committee may note a contrast between this and the age and sex groupings of the new membership, and possibly those of the membership at large. There will be no end to the many facets to explore as the pyramids are compared with each other and with the other study materials.

Pyramids of age-sex distribution, like the other study ma-

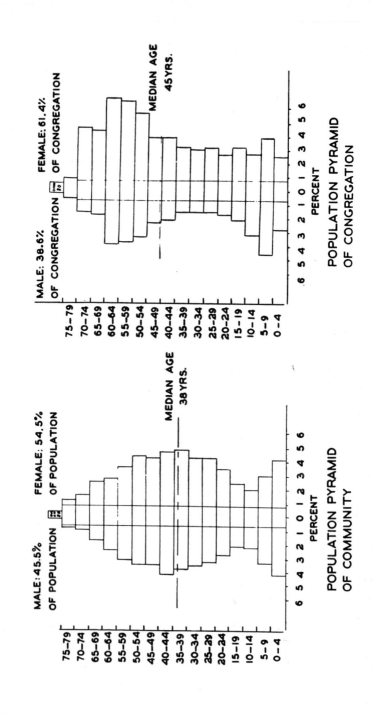

MALE: 45.5%
OF POPULATION

FEMALE: 54.5%
OF POPULATION

75—79
70—74
65—69
60—64
55—59
50—54
45—49
40—44
35—39
30—34
25—29
20—24
15—19
10—14
5—9
0—4

MEDIAN AGE
38 YRS.

6 5 4 3 2 1 0 1 2 3 4 5 6
PERCENT

POPULATION PYRAMID
OF COMMUNITY

MALE: 38.6%
OF CONGREGATION

FEMALE: 61.4%
OF CONGREGATION

MEDIAN AGE
45 YRS.

.6 5 4 3 2 1 0 1 2 3 4 5 6
PERCENT

POPULATION PYRAMID
OF CONGREGATION

terials, are essentially aids toward an understanding of the church and of its outreach and effectiveness in its community. Like the spot distribution maps or the charts of membership over the years, they are not ends in themselves, but rather thought- and question-provoking instruments, designed to foster investigation into how a church might best accomplish its work in the city situation. Accuracy of measurement should always be the goal as the committee constructs its age-sex pyramids. However, the group should also realize that at best the resultant pyramids may be only fair estimates since so few churches keep an accounting of membership by age.

The questions raised by the committee as it studies the population pyramids of its membership, new members, and leadership, against the background of the age and sex composition of the population of the community, may lead them into still other study projects. For example, should the congregational pyramid appear top-heavy with persons over fifty, which is not at all unusual for urban churches, the committee may want to see this picture in relation to the financial picture of the church. The group might construct a fourth age-sex pyramid, based on contributions by age and sex group, rather than on the total number of members. In other words the amount contributed by a single age-group of men would be divided by the total contributions to the church, and the resulting percentage charted on the appropriate bar. If the spot distribution map showed a concentration of membership in two distinct parts of the city rather than in a single area—

The population pyramid is a tool devised by the social scientist to analyze population composition of an area or an institution. The length of any bar on this chart from the center of the pyramid indicates the percentage of the total population being studied which is included within a certain age range (male population to the left, female to the right). Comparisons between congregational and community pyramids can indicate the extent of a congregation's outreach to the various age and sex groups of its community.

perhaps one gathering of members at some far end of the metropolis and another in the vicinity of the church—the self-study committee might well choose to plot the two membership concentrations as two separate pyramids, comparing them with each other and with the other pyramids of the study.

Other graphic aids

Congregations having a widely scattered membership will want to know the effects of this movement away from the church in terms of the movers retaining active membership in the church. A rather striking portrayal of the effects of movement in the city—of congregational movement—may be found in the graph of congregational mobility. Using a form similar to the chart of membership trends (except that the horizontal scale is limited to the past ten years only), three lines are plotted across the graph: the total number of active members in the church for each year; the total number of those who were active in the first year of the ten-year period and have still been active in each of the successive years; and the total number of these who each year are still living at the same address as in the first year. Time-consuming as this project may seem to be, it will prove invaluable to the study committee. The committee will be asking questions about the number of members of ten years ago who are still with the church, or about the number of these same members still with the church who have also changed addresses during the period. If through this graph it is seen that there has been an extreme turnover in membership, or an unusual degree of changing of residences on the part of those members active throughout the ten-year period, the committee will want to explore the mobility picture even further.

The two studies of congregational leadership—the spot map of leaders' residences and the age-sex pyramid of the leaders in the church—may have stirred considerable discussion among the members of the self-study group, especially as they saw them in relation to the congregational picture at large or to recent trends in new membership. The graph of congregational mobility may likewise bring new questions from the committee as to the effects of membership turnover or of membership movement upon the leadership of the church.

A bar graph of congregational leadership, indicating the number of years of membership in the church by the various leaders in the congregation, will be of further aid to the committee as it looks carefully at the leadership picture in the church. To draw this graph the committee will need to know the number of years each leader has been a member of the church. Each bar of the graph represents a grouping of so many years of membership in the church. The length of each bar is determined by the number of leaders who belong to that grouping. If, in the study of the leadership maps and pyramids, it was thought that leadership was representative of only one group in the church—perhaps the older members of the church, or possibly a newer, younger fragment of the congregation—the bar graph of congregational leadership will be of aid in determining the actual picture. This picture, in turn, should be compared with the graph of congregational mobility. The committee might look to see from what grouping, in the process of membership turnover, the leaders of the church are being selected.

Some churches may want to examine the leadership picture of the church even more carefully. They may want to chart the leadership, for example, by the number of positions held by each leader, using a similar bar graph technique in which each bar represents a specified number of positions held, and

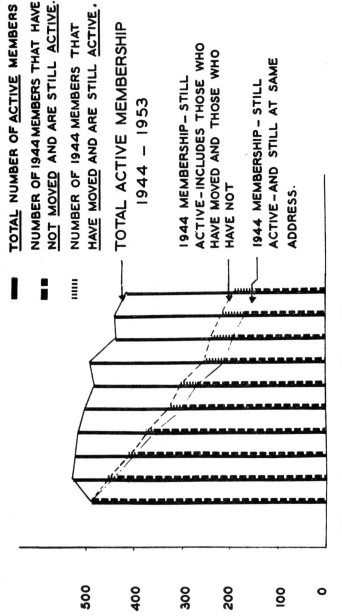

GRAPH OF CONGREGATIONAL MOBILITY

▬▬ TOTAL NUMBER OF <u>ACTIVE</u> MEMBERS

▬ ■ NUMBER OF 1944 MEMBERS THAT HAVE <u>NOT MOVED</u> AND ARE STILL <u>ACTIVE</u>.

‖‖‖‖ NUMBER OF 1944 MEMBERS THAT <u>HAVE MOVED</u> AND ARE STILL <u>ACTIVE</u>.

TOTAL ACTIVE MEMBERSHIP
1944 – 1953

1944 MEMBERSHIP – STILL ACTIVE – INCLUDES THOSE WHO HAVE MOVED AND THOSE WHO HAVE NOT

1944 MEMBERSHIP – STILL ACTIVE – AND STILL AT SAME ADDRESS.

1944 45 46 47 48 49 50 51 52 53

500

400

300

200

100

0

the length of each bar is fixed by the number of leaders holding that many positions. Another helpful aid to the committee may be a bar graph showing leadership according to the number of years for which persons have held the positions they now hold in the church.

The self-study committee may want to explore more intensively certain aspects of its congregational life revealed through analysis of the basic study aids. Perhaps in its study of the distribution maps it noted that many of the members were concentrated in several blocks, while other blocks had no church members at all. The census materials or housing surveys made available to them may have showed the committee that those blocks contrasted markedly in some way with the blocks where no church outreach was made. Perhaps the "church blocks" were areas of a high percentage of home ownership, or of high rentals, or perhaps the condition of the dwelling units was markedly better than those of nonchurch blocks. This might open the way for a study of the representativeness of the congregation in terms of income status, or employment and occupational status. Many self-study groups have found an analysis of the occupational background of their membership most useful.

Through its study of population pyramids the committee may note that a certain age group was more heavily represented in their membership than in the community itself. It would then want to delve into the matter more deeply, seeking to find what is being provided within the church for this particular age group. For example, if the church has a large

Membership in this congregation dropped from 500 to 400 over a ten-year period. At the end of this time, only 150 of the 1944 members were still active and living at the same address; another 50 of them were still active but had changed residence. In other words, 50 per cent of the congregation is new in the last ten years. Congregations need to face the implications of high mobility.

percentage of women over fifty it will want to examine the participation of these women in the various phases of the church program. Perhaps the church may find that there is actually nothing in the program for this age group of women. Similarly, if the church finds that a certain group is missing altogether in its membership, especially in the new membership of the church, it will want to look into the matter of the interests of this age group in the community. For instance, it may find that the age group of twenty to thirty is noticeably absent from their congregational picture. To find out why it might want to look both into the deficiencies of its own program and into the needs of this group as represented in the community. Contacts with these persons, consultation with other churches in the area, and discussion with local community service and social agencies will be of value as a committee seeks to make future recommendations concerning the congregation's program in these areas.

Knowing the congregation

As the committee studies its charts and maps again and again it will be uncovering areas heretofore unknown to them and to the church. The need for knowing the congregation will be stressed many times. The committee would do well to talk with many persons in the congregation as the study progresses in order to learn in greater detail the human story behind the processes which have created the patterns shown so clearly in the maps and charts. If there has been a low proportion of new members brought into the church in recent years the committee will want to know what it is that has brought these members into the church and not others. The committee might, in fact, make a careful analysis of the ways and means through which new members are brought into the church, in order to see which have been its most effective and its most ineffective methods, which need to be abandoned, or modified or further implemented.

If turnover in leadership has not followed the pace of turnover in membership, or if there are gaps in the representativeness of the church's leadership, the committee again will want to examine the factors behind this kind of development. For example, a new group of members may not be represented in the leadership of the church because it is of a racial or national background different from that of the old membership of the church. Or there may be income or status differences between the new members and the old, something that is not uncommon in the city church.

These are but a few of the facets which may be uncovered by the committee as it inquires into the underlying processes of congregational and church life. Many times it will be discovering the weaknesses in the church's life. As it looks over the charts and maps certain members may be preoccupied with these weaknesses. However, they should also be seeking out the strengths of the church and following them with the same intensity as when they pursued the underlying reasons for their weaknesses. Strengths and weaknesses can be pointed to through the various visual aids constructed by the committee. The underlying processes which create these strengths and weaknesses, however, can only be found through a knowledge of the congregation and its members within the city scene.

With a wealth of materials for study before them, and with a growing awareness of their need to know the human factors behind these materials, the committee will have plenty of work. At the same time they may want to bring together even more material and resources through which they can see their congregation and church in proper perspective. Histories of the church might be read, in which the committee might see those factors from the past which have led to the present state of affairs. Some churches have found that because of incidents in the distant past people of the community are hesitant to come into the church, even though generations have passed in the meantime. Perhaps long ago foreign-language services were conducted. Although they have since been discontinued, many in the community do not enter the church because of their feeling that this church belongs to a certain group of non-English-speaking people. Of course, many nonchurch people in looking at a church do have the feeling that it "belongs to" a certain group and newcomers don't belong. In its explorations around the community the committee might come upon this reaction.

The self-study committee might want to scrutinize carefully the materials issued by the church to its new members or prospective members. Perhaps even the wording of these materials, or the pictures contained inside, have been keeping people away. For example, the content of the literature might be portraying the church as if it were for only one particular group of people—racially, nationally, or in social and economic class. Perhaps these materials are geared to the well-educated. Perhaps they are so geared to the middle class that they keep away some persons who could add great strength to the church.

Thus far the committee may not have looked into the organizational picture of the church. In its further study it might analyze participation in the various organizations of the church in the light of the maps and charts. It might be well to see the attendance picture of the church through the recent years in the light of the graphic aids. Membership "trends" charted on the line graph, or age-sex pyramids, often tell of only one aspect of the congregation. Attendance in the church tells quite another story for many churches. Here the committee may want to compare the attendance at worship services on the part of those who are members, those who are nonmembers but regularly attending, and those who are visitors.

Again there will be no end to the useful pursuits of the study. The committee will have to be selective, choosing those pursuits which will be of most value to the ongoing work of the church. A member involved in one area of the church's life might want the committee to look more carefully into his area, even though it might not actually warrant the special attention of the committee. Finally, as the committee makes its selection of the inquiries it wishes to pursue it will want to call upon appropriate resources from the outside for assistance.

9

Where Do We Go From Here?

It is assumed that by the time a congregational study committee is seriously ready to consider the question, "Where do we go from here?" it has completed all the suggested study aids, including both the charts and maps. Likewise, it is assumed that the resource leaders from the community will have been contacted and pertinent community data carefully studied and analyzed. The church does not exist in a vacuum. It is involved in the workings of its community. Therefore, a realistic awareness of community resources, agencies, and their functions and contributions, are basic to effective urban church witness.

If a group of congregations have shared together in this study process it is assumed that the composite maps have been completed and opportunity provided for joint appraisal of this information. A comparison of the respective charts and graphs can also yield many interesting insights.

One of the first questions to come to the mind of the study committee at this juncture is, "What is our specific geographical area of responsibility?" It is not possible in the churches of American Protestantism to have a rigid set of parish boundaries that delineate the "service areas" of adjacent parishes. But we can arrive at a decision as to areas of primary responsibility, namely, those areas which are primarily the concern and the opportunity of a particular congregation. In the light of the information secured, what are the boundaries of this particular parish?

Are there concentrations of other Protestant churches which would modify some of the previous conceptions of parish boundaries? Are there natural barriers such as major thoroughfares, or industrial or commercial sections which would indicate a possible reappraisal of parish boundaries? Do there exist certain major transportation facilities which would tend to create what might be called linear rather than circular parish areas? What about the social class differences between adjacent neighborhoods? Would this suggest that perhaps a certain congregation ought to be identified with one level of society, assuming that this is also a geographical identification, and that other congregations be identified with other strata and neighborhoods? Has consideration been given to programs that might appeal to the different classes within the parish area of the church? What are the implications of these boundaries for the transfer of members into, as well as out of, each congregation? What about the distant members—what shall be the attitude of the churches to these scattered constituencies?

The picture of the community

What have been some of the major developmental stages in the life of this particular community as well as of the whole metropolitan area? Have there been certain key periods in recent history when major changes occurred, changes having specific impact on the area served by the churches? When one considers the condition of this neighborhood ten, twenty, or thirty years ago, and compares it with the neighborhood of today, what seem to be the long-range trends of the neighborhood?

At the same time that we consider the history of the neighborhood we ask: What is the history of the church in relationship to it? At what time in the neighborhood's history did this church begin? How was it related to its community? What changes have occurred in this relationship over the intervening years? To what extent was the church formerly a nationality or a class church? At what time did significant changes occur in the relationship of the church to the community and in the make-up of the church itself?

A careful study of both the land-use map and the zoning map will tell an interesting story about the neighborhood of the church. How does the use of the land today compare with the planned use of the land as indicated on the zoning map? What do the changes mean for the future of the church?

Increasingly traffic is becoming a problem for the city planner. Where shall he provide for parked cars? How shall he provide through ways for the mounting number of automobiles? The church must be mindful of both the public transportation facilities and the parking facilities for automobiles. Several churches have prepared small maps for neighborhood circulation showing the location of their church in relationship to these facilities.

A study of the housing of the neighborhood in comparison to the housing of other census tracts in the city will turn up some unique findings. How do single-family residential areas differ from duplex or apartment house areas? What kind of family groupings is one most likely to find in the different kinds of areas? What does this say with respect to the programming of the church?

In many cities composite rankings of various social and economic characteristics are tabulated for the respective neighborhoods. How does the church's neighborhood rank with respect to its metropolitan area? Considering some of the specific characteristics such as population density, rental charges, age of housing, do these factors suggest that the church ought to relocate into another area? Should it adjust its program to meet the needs of the surrounding population?

What nationality groups make up the population in the neighborhood? How does the income level in the neighborhood compare with that in adjacent neighborhoods and with the rest of the metropolitan area? Does this information offer any realistic guidance for stewardship programs in the church?

As far as the nationality distribution is concerned, should the church consider a special-language service for some newcomers to the American scene? Some study committees, after having discovered that particular nationality groups were quite heavily represented in their area, attempted to institute adult education programs geared to meet the need for these newcomers. As one gives attention to the newcomers of various nationalities it is important to consider also those in-migrants who have recently arrived from various cultural backgrounds within the American scene, such as southern whites or rural Negroes.

What of the educational level in the neighborhood? Would it indicate that more simple or more complex programs ought to be considered by the auxiliaries? Would it indicate that the make-up and content of the worship service, as well as of the educational program ought to be reconsidered?

The occupation study of the neighborhood can likewise tell a most interesting story. It has been found that the concentration of professional, managerial, and like categories is much higher in the areas more distant from the city center, whereas laboring and service personnel are concentrated close to the center of the city. This should no doubt be reflected in the scheduling of programs and activities.

The population pyramid, or age-sex distribution, of a

neighborhood is extremely significant. As one moves from the center of the city out toward the suburban fringe the median age of a neighborhood in general tends to become lower and lower. More will be said later in the chapter concerning this community information and its comparison to the congregational pyramid.

The number of families and single persons is also a revealing community characteristic. Some neighborhoods are almost completely made up of family groups, whereas others are almost totally populated by unrelated individuals, that is, by persons who are single, widowed, or divorced. The type of neighborhood it confronts means a great deal to a congregation in its programming, publicity, and outreach.

Several churches, once they discover concentrations of single people of various ages living in the neighborhood of the church, have established special auxiliary groups for them. Since people tend to associate with those who are of similar background and interests it seems wise for the church to give special consideration to the various age levels and family attachments or lack of family attachments among the people in its neighborhood.

A great deal has been said in chapters I and II about population mobility. In the city of Los Angeles, for example, the most stable neighborhoods have a mobility of approximately 20 per cent, which is the national average. In some neighborhoods we find 60 per cent of the residents moving each year. In some of the older eastern cities there are neighborhoods that have a mobility rate as low as 7 or 8 per cent. It is important that a congregation see its neighborhood and the procession of people passing through it, not only in relation to the life of the congregation, but also in relation to the life of the community. Where do these people come from? Is this a port-of-entry area? Is this one of the stopping points along the way as the people move outward from the center towards the suburbs?

Considering further the matter of mobility, are some of the people now living in this neighborhood people who have moved back into it after having once lived further out? Some experts predict a long-range trend in urban areas whereby a significant portion of the population will be moving back into the central city areas as they become rehabilitated and redeveloped. This will in no way stem the continuing tide of population flow outward from the center. It will simply mean that at the same time a reverse current will be developing.

With respect to these various community characteristics just described, a congregation should consider their impact not only on itself but on the total church in the metropolitan area. What do these factors and changes mean by way of joint programming and co-ordinated action for the churches? As programs are considered and possible staff expansion discussed, should several churches think together in terms of securing additional services, perhaps pooling resources to employ a parish worker or group worker (see chapter V)?

On an appropriately labeled map the locations of the various Protestant and Catholic churches and the Jewish synagogues ought to be indicated. It helps a congregation to be able to see its location in relation to the various religious institutions serving adjacent areas. Are there certain places which are obviously overchurched or highly churched? Are there certain other areas with no churches or relatively few churches? Does the distribution of churches have any bearing on the congregational membership?

On the same map should be located the various schools, as well as health and welfare agencies. Have the services of the neighborhood health and welfare agencies been discussed by the congregational leaders? What relationships ought to exist

between them and the churches? Have the church members
translated their Christian social responsibility into a specific
concern for their neighbors' needs? Has that concern found
avenues for concrete expression?

The picture of the congregation

A comparison of the four maps from each congregation can
be extremely helpful. Looking first at the membership map,
how are the members distributed throughout the neighborhood and adjacent areas? What are the explanations for the
various open places on the map? Do the members seem to be
clustered in spots? How is this accounted for? Does this distribution point up the need for some kind of shepherding or
zoning plan in order to provide more adequate pastoral care
for the members and in order to further Christian fellowship
amongst the members?

A look next at the Sunday school map can quickly reveal
which areas are being served most effectively and which are
being reached least effectively by the Sunday school. In comparing this map with the membership map, does there seem
to be an indication that the Sunday school is serving exclusively the children of member homes, or is the Sunday school
part of the growing edge of the church, serving many non-
member homes? Does this have implications for evangelism?
Does this indicate that perhaps the church is serving in "two
worlds," the children coming primarily from the neighborhood, and the membership coming primarily from a scattered
distance?

The third map is that of the leaders. How does the distribution of the leadership compare with that of the membership?
Does there seem to be a higher proportion of the leadership
that is living at a distance from the church? Are there certain

areas where there seem to be concentrations of leaders? What factors might account for this? Does a study of the leadership map indicate that perhaps more attention ought to be given to representation from the immediate neighborhood on the leadership level of the church? Compare the leadership map with the Sunday school map. What are some of the implications of this comparison? When leaders live at a distance they often do not have children in the Sunday school because their children have grown up and moved away from home.

A careful study of the map showing the distribution of new members received in the last ten years will indicate those areas that are being reached most effectively by the evangelism program of the church. To what extent has the neighborhood of the church been evangelized? Compare the new-membership distribution map with each of the other maps. Do a high proportion of the new members have children in Sunday school? Does this perhaps indicate that it is through the Sunday school that many of the new members are being received? Comparing again the new-members distribution map and the membership map, what similarities are there between the two? Does this perhaps indicate that new members tend to come from the areas where members live, and that where the church has not been serving in the past it continues not to serve?

Not a few churches have discovered that there is a selectivity in the outreach of their ongoing evangelism program. People tend to associate with those of similar background with respect to class and income. Their casual and informal contacts tend to be concentrated in certain areas of the city. As a result, when they invite their fellow-men to come to church with them, when they witness to the redeeming love of Christ, the congregation tends to perpetuate only its own kind. This, of course, points up the need for some kind of periodic inventory so that members can see those areas into which they are not reaching and perhaps reappraise the evangelism program in the congregation.

In the event that a group of churches have worked together in this study process and composite maps have been prepared, still another dimension of self-discovery can be considered. Many of the questions that were asked above concerning the maps of an individual congregation can now be directed to the combined maps of the participating churches. Obviously there will appear certain gaps between congregations which will point up areas of missionary concern. This is true not only in the large metropolitan centers but in the smaller cities as well.

In smaller cities it is relatively easy for a church to be situated in a central location and continue to thrive while neglecting its immediate neighborhood. In larger urban centers the scattering of members is a burden which becomes rather obvious with the passing of time. Just as in the large metropolis the inner city areas are changing, so there is also transition and adjustment in the centers of smaller cities. Congregations, therefore, need to be alerted constantly to the coverage or the outreach of their evangelism program.

Chances are that the composite map of new members received in the last ten years will tell a most interesting story for the combined churches. Does it indicate a selectivity of outreach? Why is the denomination as a whole faring so poorly in certain parts of the area? What ought the congregation to do in the light of the findings from these composite maps?

The comparison of congregational pyramids has proven to be one of the more interesting as well as revealing facets of this study process. As the congregational pyramid is placed over the community pyramid many variations will appear. It is well worth a study committee's time to spend several hours discussing the differences between the pyramids and what these differences might imply. What factors have caused these differences? What program adjustments ought to be made in the light of these differences?

For example, congregations that thought they were financially better situated than ever before, once they analyzed their pyramid, began to see that they were actually top-heavy. A significant portion of their contributions was coming from persons over fifty or fifty-five years of age. Probably in another ten or fifteen years that same high proportion of their income would no longer be available to support the budget.

Other congregations have come to realize that in their neighborhood they were not reaching the young adults of twenty to thirty-five years of age. Heretofore they had rationalized the situation by saying that there were no longer any young adults in the neighborhood. Census Bureau data, however, gave evidence to the contrary. Therefore it became apparent to these congregations that they ought to direct some particular evangelistic outreach to this age group. Inasmuch as it is often easier for a person thirty years old to be approached by another person of his own age rather than by someone considerably older, these congregations asked some of their senior citizens to serve as baby sitters while the young adults went out on evangelism calls for the church. Any number of possibilities can develop once the awareness is created, once a congregation begins to see just where it has been going.

The population pyramid, likewise, can point up the need for increased youth activities. Or it might indicate, by virtue of the number of older people both in the community and in the congregation, that a program for senior citizens is needed.

In still other situations where the discrepancy between the male and female percentage has been significant and this data has been checked with the family status statistics of the community, it became apparent that a program beamed to unrelated individuals was in order. Obviously the needs and interests of the single, unattached working girl would be quite different from that of the housewife and her family.

A comparison of the population pyramid of new members with the pyramid of the existing membership is most interesting. Congregations tend to perpetuate themselves in terms of age-sex distribution as well as national origin. If the pyramid of the new members does not show a median age slightly lower than that of the pyramid for the congregation as a whole, this is an indication that the congregation is getting older year by year as it reaches out to a constantly aging population. As in the case of the maps, so too the age-sex pyramids indicate that where a congregation is strong it tends to grow still stronger, and where it is weak it tends to grow weaker.

In studying the pyramid of leadership one needs to ask whether or not the various age levels of the congregation are represented in the policy making of the church. Is the church perhaps placing the leadership decisions strictly in the hands of the older members? Is there any connection between this fact and the pyramids of the congregational membership and of new members?

As a congregation studies the cumulative effect that mobility has upon it, it needs to consider seriously the demands that this shifting population makes upon the existing staff of the church. Not too many years ago neighborhoods were relatively stable. Today they are extremely fluid. Many churches find themselves with a turnover of far more than 50 per cent in a ten-year period. In such cases a possible increase in staff would be in order. Secretarial assistance, parish workers, educational directors—all become musts in the rapidly shifting urban scene.

The graph analyzing the distribution of leadership according to length of membership ought to be compared with the mobility chart. How long have the various leaders been members of the congregation? Assuming on the basis of the mobility chart that 50 per cent of the members are new in the last ten years, how does this compare with the leadership chart? What percentage of the leaders are from the new group in the congregation?

It might be interesting further to evaluate the leadership structure by separating the board members from those leaders who are not on the official board. Does this comparison indicate that new members are perhaps not being accepted into leadership roles as readily as they might be? Would this perhaps indicate reasons why the congregation is not adjusting to its changing neighborhood as well as it might?

Communication, involvement, and implementation

As the various pieces of community and congregational information and insight begin to fit together into a comprehensive picture over the months of the study's progress, the members of the committee will have begun to understand more clearly just what is happening both to their neighborhood and to their church. As they attempt to draw the various strands into a single comprehensive whole in order to arrive at particular plans and programs and directives for the future life of the congregation, many new doors will have opened up. It is important that the committee bear in mind the time dimension—the gradual way in which this new understanding of the situation has developed.

Some congregational committees have worked diligently over a six-month period and arrived at intelligent and far-reaching decisions for the life of the church, only to carry these suggestions and recommendations immediately to a congregational meeting and have them soundly voted down. Rather than emerging as heroes and as creative leaders they emerged as defeated and dejected dreamers. The explanation for this is rather simple. They did not realize that it takes time for a large group of individuals to begin to accept some of these disturbing and quite different viewpoints.

It is wise for the congregational committee to plan a specific program for the "communication of study findings" (how it will communicate its study findings to the congregation). Informal presentations and discussions with the various interest and auxiliary groups within the congregation are extremely worth while. Another approach which has been very effective is that of a series of "cottage meetings" (informal sessions with groups of members meeting in various homes) where representatives of the study committee are present along with the pastor. Attempts are made to interpret some of the findings to these groups, giving them ample opportunity for discussion, not trying to jump to immediate conclusions or specific program directives, but rather aiming at an understanding of the situation.

Not all persons will respond favorably to the study findings. Indecision, stubbornness, and skepticism will be expressed in many instances. Everyone should be invited to share in open and frank discussion. Divergent views must be respected and accepted in Christian love. As the guidance of the Holy Spirit is sought in these deliberations, new kinds of response to community needs may become apparent.

Many congregational committees have inserted periodic reports in the church bulletin or church newspaper, and have even had announcements made at Sunday services concerning some of the study findings. On appropriate occasions sermons have been preached relating to the responsibility of the church for its community, the relationship between the Christian faith and contemporary problems.

A congregational retreat would be helpful, to which 25, 35, of even 50 per cent of the members might be invited for discussion of various phases of this information and of other congregational concerns.

To the extent that the members of the church are involved in a kind of educational process whereby they themselves begin to think through the implications of these study findings, the plans and ideas will be carried over into action. The implementation of these study findings is important. Unless there is communication and involvement there will be no implementation.

10

A Look into the Future

The recent social changes and current developments high-lighted in the preceding chapters are momentous enough to warrant a look into the future. As we are able to analyze trends that have been and presently are operative in a situation we gain insights into possible future transitions. Church-men need continually to be alert and sensitive to the shifting scene of contemporary society, and to study its implications for present programs and future planning.

Major social trends

According to the United States Census Bureau we can expect by 1975 a possible population in the United States of 228,000,000 persons. The continuing growth in numbers, coupled with the relentless migration from rural to urban settings, indicate a forecast of perpetual change for the urban church. The Chicago metropolitan area is expected to grow at the rate of a hundred thousand a year for the next twenty years. The New York metropolitan area is presently increasing at the rate of more than six hundred every day. Such develop-ments are not occurring only in the large metropolitan areas. There are similar growth patterns in the smaller and middle-sized cities as well. Some population experts predict that cities with a sound economic base can reasonably expect a doubling of their population within the next twenty-five or thirty years. Assuming that high fertility and low mortality rates continue until the year 2000, a population of 342,673,000 might be possible for the nation as a whole by that time.[1]

Coupled with the expanding population pattern, a continuation of the present mobility rate is also expected. Automation, which is still a relatively new word in modern industry, is a portent of many significant changes for the future. A reduction of the work week and the resulting increase in leisure time are but two of the obvious by-products of automation. Increased productivity and greater leisure time can be either potential blessings or worrisome problems for urban society. As Clifton Fadiman states, "Perhaps we might be stirred to more useful action if it were made clear that wholesale leisure is not only an opportunity but a peril. Just because the word leisure has traditionally pleasant connotations we may fail to realize that it presents us with a critical as well as a novel state of affairs. It is like peace. Peace is associated with calm, rest, harmony: it sounds like a passive state. But if we should ever really be pitchforked into a universal peace we would in a daze wake up to the fact that it is a dynamic state, and that the proper use of peace necessitates the calling forth on a vast scale of human energies that have hardly been stimulated, much less tapped."[2]

He further adds, "Now free time can be used in two ways. One is play, which includes all ways of killing time. The other is engagement in leisure activities. . . . These things are engaged in for their own sakes—that is why they are not labor. Work is done under compulsion. Leisure activities, however,

[1] T. N. E. Greville, *Illustrative U. S. Population Projections* (Actuarial Study No. 46, Social Security Administration, Department of Health, Education, and Welfare, Washington: 1957), p. 23, Table 8. (This is a limited circulation report.)

[2] Clifton Fadiman, "Boredom, Brainstorms, and Bombs," *Saturday Review of Literature*, XL (August 31, 1957), 7.

we engage in freely; they are not 'externally compensated.' "[3]
New opportunities for more people to make more choices are
part of that social world whose outlines are just now emerging.
"There is nothing in free time which by itself determines
whether our citizens shall grow more conformist or various,
whether they shall attain a new dimension of freedom or
merely seek escape from a sense of purposelessness."[4]

The questions are sometimes asked: "Will not this continuing picture of mobility and the increase of leisure time,
both on the farm and in the city, bring about a kind of
'universal man'? Will the differences between the urban and
the rural inhabitant eventually disappear? Are the needs of
city people really any different from those of people living in
rural areas?"

Kenneth D. Miller speaks to these questions when he says,
"The distinction between 'city slicker' and 'country yokel' is
currently being diminished. There are certain basic common
needs the world over. Everywhere people face sorrow, sick-
ness, the need to make a living, to get along with their spouses,
rear children, grow old and die.

"Yet certain characteristics are highlighted and certain
needs intensified in the city. There is no such thing as city
man—there are city people. There are a variety of people and
needs in the city. Every city is different. Programs that will
go in one city will be a big flop in another. City people are
obsessed by the American drive to get ahead. They are lonely
and anonymous, in need of companionship. They are a
heterogeneous lot needing to discover how much they are like
others. They are under great tension to earn a living and keep
up with the schedule of the city. They move around fast and
often need help in putting down even shallow roots. They have

[3] *Ibid.*, p. 8.
[4] August Hecksher, "Time, Work, and Leisure, a Problem in American
Values," *Twentieth Century Fund Annual Report 1956* (New York), p. 15.

in their midst some of the country's greatest and gravest problems, all in one place. They have to know how to meet these problems and how to carry responsibility; they need the undergirding of their moral and spiritual life possible only through vital experience in the Christian Church."[5]

These changes and the related problems of urban individuals and their communities have attracted attention on every hand. One finds leaders in many fields speaking of the need for a vital concern for our urban centers. As George Kennan said in his Stafford Little Lectures, stressing the international meaning of domestic problems, "Blighted areas, filthy streets, community demoralization, juvenile delinquency, chaotic traffic conditions, utter disregard for aesthetic and recreational values in urban development, and an obviously unsatisfactory geographic distribution of various facilities for home life and work and recreation and shopping and worship; these things may not mark all our urban communities in conspicuous degree; but they mark enough of them to put a definite imprint that leads others to feel that we are not really the masters of our own fate, that our society is not really under control, that we are being helplessly carried along by forces we do not have the courage or the vitality to master. . . . Peoples of the world are not going to be inclined to accept leadership from a country which they feel is drifting in its own internal development and drifting into bad and dangerous waters."[6]

Leading theologians also are adding their voices in support of this concern. They are calling on the church to proclaim the gospel vigorously, rather than merely to defend it, and to apply it in new ways to modern society. The church, they

[5] Quoted by R. W. Sanderson in *Toward Better City Churches* (New York: Urban Department, N.C.C.C.U.S.A., 1955), pp. 37–38.
[6] Philip C. Jessup, "Ends and Means of American Foreign Policy," *International Stability and Progress: United States Interests and Instruments* (New York: The American Assembly, Graduate School of Business, Columbia University, 1957), p. 19.

say, must confront the total needs of the total individual. "A person, therefore, must be dealt with in his entirety and in his specific need," says Martin J. Heinecken. "He who is a Christ to him must help him with the gifts he actually possesses. If he is hungry he must feed him, provided he has food to give. If he is sick, he must give him medicine and care, provided he has the medicine and the 'know how.' If he is the victim of social injustice with which no individual can possibly cope alone, then he must set in motion the machinery our democratic setup still fortunately provides in order to change the situation. This means making use of all the agencies, skills and enlightened methods the twentieth century provides. He must endeavor to bring into play whatever the moment demands to relieve the need."[7]

Heinecken further adds, "Since a man is constituted by his relations, it is necessary not only to change the God-relationship, but also the other relations in which human beings live. Therefore, housing and living conditions may be such that they will require social action in order to change those relations in which it is impossible for human beings to live as human beings. Juvenile delinquents may be made such by the conditions under which they live in much the same way that water is converted into steam or ice quite depending upon the temperature."[8]

In surveying contemporary needs the church must not limit its activities to those areas which will yield the immediate reward of inflated statistics on the membership rolls. Rather, it must serve in response to need simply because the need exists. Speaking to the responsible Christian, Dr. Heinecken con-

[7] Martin J. Heinecken, "Historical and Theological Involvement of the Lutheran Church in Social Welfare," *Proceedings of Regional Meetings, 1956, Lutheran Welfare Conference in America*, pp. 3–4. Speech delivered at the Atlantic-Central Regional Meeting, New York, May 8–9, 1956.

[8] *Ibid.*, p. 14.

tinues, "The church has only *one task*, to minister to the world with the Gospel, to exercise its universal priesthood. This means that you do what is needed and you always serve with whatever you possess. You feed the hungry because they are hungry and not because of some ulterior motive. In the parable of the Good Samaritan we are not told that the Samaritan loaded the Jew with tracts or dinned his ear with a proselytic appeal, while he held him as a captive audience strapped fast to his ass. But he simply did what the moment required."[9]

Congregational planning

A perpetual tendency in institutions—and the church is not exempt from this—is to let a specific program crystallize and then to perpetuate it on the basis of habit or of vested interest rather than to examine it periodically to consider its current relevance and validity. Even in a relatively stable situation it is important that the ongoing work should be analyzed and appraised now and then. In the midst of urban change such analysis becomes even more imperative. New insights may be learned, new techniques developed and new forms of service designed which might well bring about improvements in programming.

Churches would do well to keep many of their organizations and group activities on a flexible and adaptable basis. Perhaps this year a certain program needs to be instituted. Possibly next year it will have to be discontinued and something else tried. Some people feel that to discontinue a program means that the program has failed. It is far more valid to assume that the need for that particular program no longer exists.

In order that this kind of appraisal and planning might

[9] *Ibid.*, p. 15.

actually take place in the church, it is considered worth while for a congregation to have a committee charged with the specific responsibility of planning. Included in this committee's responsibility might well be the periodic appraisal of every program in the church. Then, too, it would be well to keep a continuing study of the neighborhood and of the total community in process. Pertinent reports from various municipal and welfare agencies ought to be studied. Conferences with key resource leaders from the community might be held occasionally. It would be the job of this committee to have an "overview" of congregational life as it relates to the community.

A periodic door-to-door canvass or census of the area around the church is important. The turnover of population in the urban neighborhood merits this expenditure of manpower and money. This obviously would be the job of the congregation's evangelism committee. Yet the planning committee would certainly have a responsibility for the timing of this effort.

More attention needs to be given to the involvement of congregational members in the policy making and programming of the congregation. Greater effort needs to be made in stirring up give-and-take discussion within the congregation. (See the Appendices, pages 174–175, for some "Suggestions for Fostering Discussion in the Study Process.")

Perhaps every five years, or even oftener, groups of churches might work together in a formal urban church study program along the line of the methods described in this text. The social problems and particular needs of the neighborhood need to be appraised constantly. If leisure-time services for youth or aged are to be provided or expanded, for example, the church ought to become informed about new education or group-work methods. What does a group worker do? How would a youth group under the direction of such a worker differ from the more traditional youth fellowship activity in the church? Information about such programs can and ought to be secured from reliable leaders in the community.

Just as it is important that there be maintained an adaptability in the programming of a congregation, so it is essential that there be room for flexibility in the physical plant. Sanctuaries and educational units that are built in the early days of a new community are called upon to meet the needs of a population that is relatively young and has a very high proportion of children and young adults. With the passing years the population composition of the neighborhood will change (see chapter VIII). The pyramid of the community begins to indicate a higher percentage of teen-agers and middle-aged adults. Then, as the community comes into its "mature years," one finds that there is a larger proportion of senior citizens and older adults whose children have married and gone to live elsewhere. Thus the demands upon a church plant over the years will vary with the changing population structure.

It goes without saying that before any investments in plant are made a thorough study of the community ought to be undertaken. There are some urban churches, sad to say, that have actually built large plants as a dying gesture of their last remaining strength. Would that they had spent greater sums on personnel and programming rather than on the buildings themselves!

In contemplating the future plant of a congregation oftentimes a gymnasium is considered. There was a time—perhaps twenty or thirty years ago—when it was felt that every church ought to have a gymnasium. Today, however, the opinion prevails in most circles that the gymnasium facilities ought to be and are being adequately provided by such agencies as schools, the Y.M.C.A and Y.W.C.A., and recreation agencies serving the entire community; that the churches need rather to provide space for meetings of small groups of various kinds.

Another responsibility of the planning committee might be consideration of staff expansion. In larger churches it is especially important that job responsibilities and descriptions be clearly delineated and defined. Not only are most urban churches woefully understaffed, but when they do have multiple staffs they often are lacking in clear-cut designation of responsibilities. As a minimum every urban pastor ought to be freed of many of the secretarial and office responsibilities which could be handled by a qualified secretary. If the church is unable to afford a full-time secretary for its pastor, certainly arrangements ought to be made for a part-time secretary. Possibly this might be accomplished by several churches pooling resources to hire a secretary who could serve their common purposes.

If urban churches are to be properly staffed in the future, especially in the light of the acute shortage of trained pastors, then greater opportunity must be provided for the training and preparation of interested laymen to enter full-time church service. Opportunities for business managers, youth workers, parish education directors, secretaries, and others, are not nearly as unusual as they once were. Today they are opening up on every hand. Therefore, channels for the recruiting, training, and hiring of such persons ought to be expanded.

The question of "optimum size" should be a serious consideration of every growing congregation. How large ought a church to be? Does bigness always mean strength? At what point does a church begin to serve less effectively? Can a congregation really minister to an area as large as the one it has allocated to itself, or should it perhaps serve a more limited field and foster the establishment of a new mission congregation?

Though there are no clear-cut answers to the above questions, they do need to be considered. When a congregation exceeds five hundred adult members a different kind of relationship develops among the parishioners. Many are total strangers to other members. Smaller groupings within the larger group become evident. Efforts to promote loyalty and cohesion within the congregation require more deliberate thought. When can a church serve most effectively—when it has a thousand, fifteen hundred, or two thousand members? This involved question may be answerable only on an individual basis. We have tried simply to suggest that unlimited growth may present problems, including that of pride in sheer size.

The congregation needs constantly to criticize itself if it is honestly to evaluate its effectiveness. The genius of the Christian church—indeed, its vindication—is evident in the forceful criticism that comes from within its own ranks. A striking note is sounded by the layman who warns that over-emphasis on activity may keep the church from performing its unique role. The suburban-type church member "can be galvanized into action-type programs upon presentation of evidence that his children do not have adequate Sunday school space. But, God help us, these are not his *real* problems, nor are they the real problems of his children. . . . This is no quarrel with the institution of the church nor with the need for physical plant. It is a plea to the church that it bring to society a new spiritual leadership to establish those relationships of man to man and that concept of society which are wholly inherent in beliefs which Christians profess."[10]

William H. Whyte, Jr., in his recent best seller, *The Organization Man,* reports the viewpoint of a Protestant chaplain

[10] Perry L. Norton, "The Role of the Church in the Community," *The City Church,* VII (May–June, 1956), 16, 19.

called by a council of churches to organize a new church in a rapidly growing "package community" outside one of our large metropolitan cities: "He wanted a *useful* church, and to emphasize theological points, he felt, was to emphasize what is not of first importance and at the price of provoking dissension. 'We try not to offend anybody,' he explains."[11]

According to Mr. Whyte, this chaplain found that the mobility of residents in this new community had weakened their denominational ties. "In moving from one community to another, many of the transients had gone where there was either no church of their faith or one that to them seemed mediocre, and as a consequence they had got in the habit of 'shopping.' "[12]

And speaking of shopping, Stanley Rowland, Jr., a religious news reporter for the *New York Times,* wrote an article in *The Nation* entitled, "Suburbia Buys Religion." He suggested that the flocking of newer suburbanites to churches and synagogues indicates a drive for cultural and religious identification. He went on to note that "the main mood of many a suburban church on Sunday is that of a fashionable shopping center. This is cultural identification on a wide, superficial and generally unacknowledged level. On weekdays one shops for food, on Saturday one shops for recreation, and on Sunday one shops for the Holy Ghost."[13]

"In some ways the visible church in America," writes William Miller, "is peculiarly susceptible to the evil of groupism: the compulsions of its bureaucratic apparatus may be cloaked in doctrines of the church, and the demands and seductions of the local 'fellowship' may be heightened by its claim to be

[11] William H. Whyte, Jr., *The Organization Man,* p. 406.
[12] *Ibid.,* p. 407.
[13] Stanley Rowland, Jr., "Suburbia Buys Religion," *The Nation,* July 28, 1956, p. 79. See also Waldo Beach, "Euphoria in Suburbia," *Christianity and Crisis,* XVI (April 2, 1956), 33–34.

the agency of higher things. Whyte (*The Organization Man*) has a chapter on the church in his section on life in a suburban development, and a very fellowshipy operation it is: it seems almost a contemporary theologian's satire on what a church ought not—primarily—to be, above all 'socially useful,' striving not to offend anybody, subordinating doctrine to the needs of friendliness, built around the personality of the minister and the accessibility of the Sunday School.

"But the self needs its communities, and the eagerness for 'belonging' and 'togetherness' in our time is not altogether to be dismissed; rather its corruptions are to be attacked in order that the self's true need for a community of warmth, acceptance and cooperative effort may be more nearly realized."[14]

Intercongregational planning

In the chapters dealing with community organization and planning (chapters II and IV) it was indicated that there is a complex network of interrelating organizations operative in the American city. The individual as well as the group must recognize the vast influence of such social structures in urban life. Above all there is the tendency toward concentrations of power, often interlocking, of economic and political sorts. The power structure of a community is a reality to be reckoned with in considering the possibilities of change or improvement through planned, co-operative efforts. Awareness that control is from the top down in a given community should preclude any naive assumptions as to what can be accomplished there; however, it need not mean yielding to defeatism. There are often latent forces that can be mobilized. Churchmen may even hold the key to new kinds of power to challenge the

[14] William Lee Miller, "The Organization and the Individual," *Christianity and Crisis*, XVII (June 24, 1957), 85.

entrenched positions.[15] But to do this congregations must work together.

In the final analysis, no individual, group, or congregation is unrelated to the entire community structure and to the various components within it. In the light of this fact it may be in order to re-evaluate the extreme emphasis on local autonomy which is to be found in some congregations. Each congregation must evaluate itself, of course, in terms of its "constituency responsibility." But it must also plan with regard for the needs of the total community and for the total impact of the whole church upon the total city. It is not enough for a congregation to plan merely on the basis of what it wants for itself. Rather, it must see itself in the larger context of evangelical Christianity as a whole confronting the changing urban scene, and appraise its own role in the light of the broad mission of the total church. For example, can the last few "die-hards" in a given urban congregation deny the Christian message to those in its neighborhood who need to know Christ as Lord and Savior? Can a congregation locate its buildings or alter its plant and program in complete ignorance of the plans of near-by churches, and yet continue to assume that it is serving most effectively?

There is an urgent need for closer co-ordination of effort among the denominations and within the respective denominations themselves. To foster local community awareness of and involvement in planning, denominations within local urban areas ought to have some kind of denominational planning council. This council could aid the congregations in appraising their changing situation, in determining the location of new missions, and in fostering closer working relationships among the congregations of the denomination.

Councils of churches have proven extremely helpful in

[15] Arthur Hillman, *Sociology and Social Work*, pp. 45–46.

bringing a more co-ordinated impact to bear on an urban community. Research and study ought to become increasingly a part of their responsibility—a service to council members and a channel for participation in over-all community planning. In the smaller councils of churches it would obviously have to be a part-time responsibility for some staff member. In larger urban centers the council could well use a full-time planning person on the staff. In the very large urban centers a multiple staff, devoted exclusively to church planning, co-ordination, and strategy ought to be the rule.

Planners, renewal leaders, welfare councils and other related agencies are asking that the churches work in closer co-ordination with them. The church has a responsibility to relate itself to these agencies and to strengthen their work in the community. It is almost impossible for separate denominations, much less separate congregations, to do this in an effective way. Not only can the work of such agencies be augmented by the support and counsel of the churches, but the very work of the churches themselves can be made far more effective through such co-operation.

To describe and to foster this kind of teamwork Meryl Ruoss has listed some steps for developing a strategy for church involvement in urban redevelopment: "One, comprehensive and intensive analysis of present situations and projected programs. . . . Two, . . . a long-range view of the breath-taking opportunities and responsibilities of the next twenty-five to forty years. . . . Three, set goals as Christian individuals and groups—denominationally and interdenominationally. . . . Four, partnership participation in the city-planning process. . . . Five, partnership participation in actual programs of building and rebuilding. . . . Six, a realistic policy formulation process which studies interrelatedness of city church needs and develops and allocates resources accordingly. . . .

Seven, develop contemporary administrative structures adequate to analyze, plan, develop policy and implement."[16]

As congregations take seriously their responsibility to their changing neighborhoods, some of the insights of the professional welfare worker can be of significant value to the church. Those denominations which are fortunate enough to have related to their structure a group of professionally qualified social workers ought to make use of such persons in assisting their urban congregations. Understanding and techniques of group work can be learned from them for use with the various age levels. Some of the church-related welfare agencies might establish services to congregations, possibly having personnel devote full time to counseling congregations in the establishment of specific programs. Already there are many encouraging signs of this new kind of working relationship between congregations and social welfare. Many new possibilities still remain to be discovered.

Denominational planning

At the national level Protestant denominations today can be of considerable assistance to the urban pastor and his congregation. It is sometimes rather difficult to achieve a comprehensive understanding of neighborhood changes in urban communities without having access to an overview of various cities. Through the channels of the denominational structure it is possible to communicate understanding and know-how amongst congregations of various urban communities.

Positive principles and directives from the denomination can be of real support to the urban congregation as it attempts to minister and serve in its particular setting. In-service train-

[16] Meryl Ruoss, "The Church's Viewpoint," *The City Church,* VIII, No. 3 (May–June, 1957), 14–15.

ing institutes for pastors, and for laymen as well, can be of considerable value. When one considers that the pastor of an urban congregation often is experiencing life in the city for the first time, some kind of orientation program for him is warranted. Then too, each urban center is different from every other. There are particular resources, institutions, and factors present in the community which will require a great deal of time for the newcomer to understand and identify. Therefore it would be wise to provide orientation sessions for all new pastors and congregational leaders as they assume their new duties, perhaps in the fall of each year.

The seminary training of pastors ought to include a background in urban sociology and the processes and structure of urban life. It has been said by some, "Our seminaries concentrate all of their effort on the 'ammunition' that will be used by the pastor but pay no attention whatsoever to his future 'target'." It is hoped that before too long all seminary training will include as part of its core curriculum the study of urban society. Particular attention must be given to the needs of city dwellers who constitute the bulk of our population and of the missionary potential today.

Dr. Samuel W. Blizzard, Professor of Religion and Society at Princeton University, has been conducting a most interesting study of the changing role of the contemporary minister. He concludes a report on "The Minister's Dilemma" with this paragraph: "No matter how different ministers' ideas of what is important in the ministry, all wind up doing substantially the same thing. It is perfectly apparent how largely the social roles of Protestant parish ministers are conditioned and defined by the requests of parishioners, the denominational program and the culture of the community. It is not nearly so clear at the parish level, however, how much a minister's religious ideology or normative orientation has to do with what he actually does as a minister. Furthermore, there appear to be basic ambiguities in the church structure itself. The minister is urged to spend much time organizing and administering programs. The national church body is at the same time failing to give him an adequate theological understanding of these offices. That is the minister's dilemma."[17]

Not only do pastors need opportunity for formal study of the areas discussed in this book, but there is also need among the clergy for counseling opportunities for themselves. Especially in the neighborhoods of rapid social change some means or structure is needed whereby small groups of pastors can come together "to bear one another's burdens" and to discuss their particular parish or personal problems with a trained and sympathetic counselor. The role conflict referred to by Dr. Blizzard is a part of the problem. The rapid changes of urban life is another facet. Many complex and conflicting pressures are brought to bear on the busy city minister of today. His spiritual welfare must be a concern of the church at large.

In some of the extremely difficult urban parishes it might be that a five-year rotation plan would be called for rather than an unlimited tenure of service. To place a man with school-age children in some of the very blighted neighborhoods is to make his ministry almost impossible because of the many concerns he will have for the welfare of his children.

On the other hand, the church-at-large must be ready to evaluate on a basis different from the usual statistical yardstick the effectiveness of a man's service in such areas. Too often it has been glibly stated that a pastor can establish a self-supporting, flourishing, and growing congregation in any

[17] Samuel W. Blizzard, "The Minister's Dilemma," *The Christian Century*, April 25, 1956, p. 509. Copyright 1956 by Christian Century Foundation. Reprinted by permission from *The Christian Century*.

neighborhood in the city if he will only work hard enough. Such statements to not reflect a realistic appraisal of church work in the more difficult neighborhoods.

Financial subsidy will have to play an increasingly important part in the urban strategy of the denomination. Some congregations will have to be assisted temporarily. Others might even need continuing subsidy. It must not be made a matter of disgrace for a congregation to be aided in serving areas which might otherwise be denied the witness of the gospel.

There are many new possibilities for the planning of the denomination as it confronts the urban situation. These possibilities, however, will not become apparent unless there is first a humble and critical attitude.

"In the rational world of today certainly nothing can be done without planning, but one must beware of wanting to organize and plan the work of the Holy Spirit, for he has his majesty precisely in not being drawn into even the most pious of programs, but in moving according to his sovereign will. That we are prepared to place our technical knowledge and our rational ability in his service; that we in this obedience have better and deeper insight into the changing orders and institutions of our world than those who would shut out the idea of God as a disturbing factor; that we do our service in relation to this changing world, not in the name of man, and certainly not in the name of piety, but in the name of a gracious God—these should be some of the reflections which we make when we ask about the prerequisites of being the church in the present-day world. How few or how many of these prerequisites are fulfilled today, anyone may discover for himself."[18]

One of the factors which has contributed so markedly to

[18] Hans Bolewski, "Church and Nation," *Lutheran World*, IV, No. 1 (June, 1957), 103.

the wide interest in the work of the Evangelical Academies in Germany is their emphasis on an open and frank confrontation with the different problems of the modern world. Dr. Bolewski writes, "This type of Christianity maintains a critical attitude toward institutional Christianity; this it does partly out of the feeling of necessity, but partly also with a certain pride. But in any case it wishes to be taken seriously as Christian faith and not merely as a type of general religiosity. It may be that this community (the Academy) really has a special part to play in the affairs of our time."[19]

Whether the plans be made at the congregational, intercongregational, denominational, interdenominational or community level, the Holy Spirit can and does provide new insights and understanding to those who truly seek his guidance. The tools of the social sciences can contribute much to the intelligent study and planning of the church of Jesus Christ. As dedicated pastors and laymen prayerfully seek to know the guidance of their Lord in the midst of changing urban America, the work of the kingdom can become still more effective—helping to redeem the city dweller and his environment.

[19] Hans Bolewski, "The Ecumenical Movement and the Work of the Evangelical Academies in Germany," *Lutheran World,* III, No. 4 (March, 1957), 344.

Appendices

RECOMMENDED STUDY AIDS

The following study aids, described more fully in chapters VII and VIII, are suggested for each congregation participating in a study project:

Group I: maps

1. *Membership* distribution spot map.
2. Translucent overlay spot map of the active *Sunday school* members fourteen years of age or less.
3. Translucent overlay spot map of all church *leaders* presently serving in the congregation (Sunday school teachers and officers, auxiliary officers, board members, etc.).
4. Translucent overlay spot map of all *new members* received in the last ten years who are still active in the church.

Group II: charts

1. Age-sex pyramid of the *membership* of the congregation.
2. Chart of *membership trends* over the past thirty years.
3. *Sunday school* enrolment chart (indicating cradle roll enrolment, and total enrolment for a thirty-year period).
4. Graph indicating *financial trends* over the past thirty years in current, benevolence, and special funds.
5. Age-sex pyramid of the *new members* received in the last ten years who are still active.
6. Age-sex pyramid of the total *leadership* of the congregation.
7. Analysis of the congregational leadership in terms of *how long the various leaders have been active adult members* of the congregation.
8. Graph of congregational *mobility*.
9. Chart indicating the *methods by which the new members* received in the last five years *were first contacted*.

APPENDIX II

STEPS IN THE CONSTRUCTION OF COMPOSITE MAPS AND RELATED STATISTICAL DATA

Materials needed

The base map used by the individual congregations in their spot maps

Five sheets of translucent paper, the size of the base map

Colored pencils—black, green, red, orange, and blue

The congregational spot maps

Census tract outline map

Population statistics by census tract

Census tract outline overlay

If the base map and the census tract outline map are not of the same size and scale, as is often the case, then a census tract outline overlay should be prepared which will be of the same size and scale as the base map. On the first sheet of translucent paper, laid over the base map, outline the census tracts with a rather heavy blue line; identify a sufficient number of streets and natural boundaries so this overlay can be easily and correctly placed over the base map and congregation maps (any additional identifying lines to be lightly drawn in). In blue pencil also number the census tracts on the overlay.

Composite membership overlay

Place the second translucent sheet over the base map, and lightly draw in enough of the streets to enable it to be correctly oriented to the census tract outline overlay, the base map, and the maps submitted by he congregations. Label this overlay in the lower right corner, "Composite Membership Map," and indicate the names of the congregations submitting membership maps. Place this overlay on top of each congregation's membership map, one church after the other, copying onto the composite the dots and church locations. Use the black pencil for this map, being careful to keep each dot separate, since each dot must be counted later. Line up the composite accurately with each congregation map so the location of dots will be accurate. You have now constructed the "Composite Membership Map"—a picture of all members in this area belonging to the co-operating churches.

Composite new members overlay

Place the third translucent sheet over the base map, and lightly draw in enough of the streets so that it can be matched with the congregational "new members" spot maps and the base map. Label this overlay in the lower right corner, "Composite New Members Map," and indicate the names of the congregations submitting new members maps. Place this overlay on top of each congregation's new members map, one church after the other, copying onto the composite overlay the dots and the church locations. Use a green pencil for the dots on this map, being careful to keep each dot separate, since each dot must be counted later. Line up the composite accurately with each congregation map so the location of dots will be accurate. You have now constructed the "Composite New Members Map."

Composite leadership overlay
Place the fourth translucent sheet over the base map, and lightly draw in enough of the streets so it can be matched with the congregational "leaders" spot maps and the base map. Label this overlay in the lower right corner, "Composite Leadership Map," and indicate the names of the congregations submitting leadership maps. Place this overlay on top of each congregation's leaders map, one church after the other, copying onto the composite overlay the dots and the church locations. Use a red pencil for the dots on this map, being careful to keep each dot separate, since each dot must be counted later. Line up the composite accurately with each congregation map so the location of dots will be accurate. You have now constructed the "Composite Leadership Map."

Composite Sunday school overlay
Place the fifth translucent sheet over the base map, and lightly draw in enough of the streets so it can be matched with the congregational "Sunday school" spot maps and the base map. Label this overlay in the lower right corner, "Composite Sunday School Map," and indicate the names of the congregations submitting Sunday school maps. Then place this overlay on top of each congregation's "Sunday school" map, one church after the other, copying onto the composite overlay the dots and church locations. Use an orange pencil for the dots on this map, being careful to keep each dot separate, since each dot must be counted later. Line up the composite accurately with each congregation map so the location of dots will be accurate. You have now constructed the "Composite Sunday School Map."

A large worksheet shall then be ruled off in several columns as per the sample on page 169.
The census figures for 1950 will doubtless be available to you.

From these figures the population over fourteen years of age, and fourteen years and under, can easily be determined for each census tract.

The number of members, new members, leaders, and Sunday school pupils are secured by counting the dots in each census tract on the appropriate composite, by laying the composite over the census tract outline overlay first constructed. (Should you discover a tremendous number of dots in any one census tract, you may wish to go back to the congregation maps, placing them over the census tract outline map, and do the counting in installments.)

Calculation of all other columns can then proceed. Be sure to watch the decimal point (number/10,000 in most cases, not a percentage). Then crosscheck the figures. For example, on the sample worksheet (next page), the number of members/10,000 adult population comes out to 11. Multiply this by 1.6, the number of 10,000's there are in the total adult population, and you should get 18.

Census Tract	69
1950 Population	23,826
1950 Pop. Over 14 Yrs. of Age	16,700
Number of Members	18
# Members/ 10,000 Adult Pop.	11
Number of New Members	3
# New Memb. /10,000 Adult Pop.	2
Number of Leaders	2
# Leaders /100 Members	11
1950 Pop. 14 Yrs. Old and Under	7,126
Number of Sunday School Pupils	4
# S.S. Pupils /10,000 Pop. 14 Yrs. & Under	6

_____ Self-Study

_____ (Date)

(City) _____

APPENDIX III

SUGGESTED TIMETABLE FOR A CONGREGATIONAL AND DISTRICT SELF-STUDY

It is assumed that the study will be conducted by a group of congregations together. This group will be referred to as the study district. A five-month series of meetings is here outlined. It is suggested that each month there be a meeting within the congregation of its own study committee, and that there also be a joint meeting of all the congregational study committees in the district. Resource speakers at the joint meetings might include such persons as the city planner, the urban renewal director, a university sociologist and someone engaged in social welfare research.

First month

Congregation

1. Inform committee appointees of the background of the study, its general method, purpose, and scope.
2. Discuss problems and issues confronting the congregation.
3. Plan for participation in district meeting.
4. Distribute copies of this book to each committee member— suggest reading chapters I, VI, and VII as preparation for the district meeting.

District

1. Introduce various congregational study committee members to the group.
2. Present briefly the background, method, scope and purpose of the study.
3. Show the film, "The City Story." °
4. Discuss the film and chapters I, VI, and VII of this book.
5. Distribute study materials (maps and translucent paper).
6. Assign the four maps (chapter VII, pp. 100-104) for each congregational study committee to prepare before the next meeting.
7. Assign the reading of chapters II, III, and VIII in this book.

° A 44-minute black-and-white film available from most local film distribution centers. The National Council of the Churches of Christ in the United States of America, producer of the film, describes it thus: "The story of any city, the hopes and promises it presents. The changes which moving populations make, the economic and cultural backgrounds which also change. To these problems a pastor brings clear vision and spiritual courage. He challenges his people to stay and meet the needs of the changing community."

Second month
Congregation

1. Prepare congregational maps as assigned by district meeting.
2. Discuss information revealed by these maps.
3. Review district meeting.
4. Discuss chapters II, III, and VIII of this book.

District

1. Provide opportunity for several congregational committees to display and interpret their maps.
2. Have a talk by a resource leader from the community.
3. Discuss his presentation.
4. Assign the three line graphs, three pyramids, and mobility chart (chapter VIII, pp. 115-124) for each congregational study committee to prepare before the next meeting.
5. Discuss chapters already assigned in this book.
6. Arrange for preparation of composite maps in time for the next district meeting (see Appendix II).
7. Assign the reading of chapters IV and V in this book.

Third month
Congregation

1. Prepare charts as assigned by district meeting.
2. Discuss previous district meeting and chapters IV and V of this book.
3. Evaluate congregational charts.

District

1. Provide opportunity for presentation and discussion of several sets of congregational charts.
2. Have a presentation by another community resource person.
3. Discuss his presentation and chapters IV and V of this book.
4. Present and interpret the composite maps.
5. Arrange for reproduction of congregational charts in quantity.
6. Discuss and make plans for final workshop to be held in fifth month (see Appendix IV).
7. Assign chapters IX and X of this book for congregational reading.

Fourth month
Congregation

1. Discuss the previous district meeting.
2. Consider the implications of this study for congregational program and planning.
3. Discuss possible implementation of the study.

4. Discuss communication of the study findings to the rest of the congregation.

District
1. Distribute all congregational charts to all study committees.
2. Provide opportunity for discussion of insights gained in various congregational study committees.
3. Have a presentation by another community resource person.
4. Discuss his presentation and chapters IX and X of this book.
5. Finalize plans for the workshop of the following month.
6. Suggest rereading of entire text.

Fifth month
Congregation
1. Review maps and charts.
2. Review district meeting discussions.
3. List specific problems, opportunities, and insights related to the life of the congregation and to this study.
4. Prepare for the final workshop.

District
The Final Workshop.
It has proven extremely valuable for congregational committees to meet together for an extended period of time as a means of climaxing such a study process. Resource persons for the workshop may include leading urban pastors, jurisdictional and mission leaders, and pastors who have had an opportunity to participate in a similar study project on a previous occasion.

APPENDIX IV

SUGGESTED AGENDA FOR A FINAL STUDY WORKSHOP
(Experience has shown that 9:00 A.M. through 4:00 P.M. on Saturday are generally the best hours for congregational study committees to schedule their final workshop.)

9:00-9:15 *Opening devotions*

9:15-9:30 *"A Responsible Church":* This presentation should emphasize the responsibility of the church for its community, the social setting in which it is ministering.

9:30-10:00 *A Review of Self-study Findings:* A person who has had considerable experience in previous congregational and community studies should fill this assignment on the program. It would be his responsibility to summarize the over-all study findings and to indicate points of special concern which the groups might handle in their discussion sessions to follow.

10:00-12:00 *Congregational Discussion Groups:* A resource leader (some person who has worked with previous congregational study groups) is assigned to each congregation or to each two or three congregations. During this period he assists them in the analysis and interpretation of their own study materials in the light of the data for the community as a whole. Also he helps them to pinpoint specific recommendations and courses of action which their individual congregations ought to take.

12:00-12:15 *Report from each of the congregational groups to the general assembly.*

12:15-1:30 *Lunch*

1:30-1:45 *"Bringing the Gospel to All People":* This presentation ought to underline the inclusiveness of the Christian gospel and the fact that Christ died as Savior for *all* men.

1:45-2:00 *"Where Do We Go from Here?":* A resumé of the morning's developments should be given together with an indication of the kinds of concerns which the interest groups might have in the following hour. The interrelatedness, the togetherness of the congregations ought to be emphasized. Also, the importance of communicating this information to the grass roots of the congregation should be stated at this time.

2:00-3:30 *Special-interest Groups* (Various groupings of the workshop participants have been tried. It is important to bring together representatives of the different congregations on the basis of common interests.) Some of the interest categories are Pastors and Church Councils, Parish Education, Women of the Church, Church Youth, Men of the Church, Evangelism, Stewardship, Social Welfare.

It is suggested that the participants be limited to 10 or 15 persons per group and that a resource leader be assigned to each of the groups. The purpose of this discussion period is to provide opportunity for a review of the study findings concerning the various congregations and the community and the bearing these findings have on their particular interest, or their special responsibility.

3:30-3:45 *Report from each of the interest groups to the general assembly.*

3:45-4:00 *Report of the Findings Committee* (This is a three-man committee of selected leaders from the local area who are asked to draw together and summarize the findings from the various congregational and interest groups and to prepare a general report to the participating congregations.)

4:00 *Adjournment*

APPENDIX V

SUGGESTIONS FOR FOSTERING DISCUSSION IN THE STUDY PROCESS

Prepared by Morris L. Haimowitz
Director of the University of Chicago Human Relations Center

1. More discussion occurs in small groups than in large groups. More people can talk; the timid have less fear of being squelched.
2. Where groups must be large, train the leaders so they will know how to encourage maximum participation in the discussions.
3. Use audio-visual aids, charts, maps, graphs, blackboard.
4. Allow plenty of time for a question period; prepare the audience to be thinking of questions.
5. Give everyone an opportunity to express his views.
6. Recognize that in fruitful discussions there may even be silent periods when nobody is speaking but meaningful communication is nonetheless being carried on, through gestures or other means.
7. Develop the art of sympathetic listening.
8. Foster responsibility on the part of the group, urging the people themselves to assume leadership in discussing, deciding, and acting.
9. Encourage expression of the least articulate by:
   a) Asking the group if any other views might be expressed
   b) Calling on nonspeakers, but only when they show signs of wanting to speak
10. Have favorable physical arrangements for two-way discussion:
    a) People seated in small groups
    b) People seated as close together as possible but not uncomfortably close
    c) Round tables rather than long tables or row seating, if the group numbers fewer than 20 participants
    d) Fresh air at comfortable temperature
    e) Adequate lighting
11. Leaders ought to be sensitive to the "hidden responses" of their

group members. Even in a lecture situation the speaker can be sensitive to such signs as the nodding of heads and restlessness.

12. Leaders should discuss programming with the various age and interest groups in the congregation. If they have helped prepare the program they will be interested in how it develops.

13. Age groups from sixteen to twenty-four seem to be segregated and noncommunicative with older age groups. Special efforts might be made to bring them into planning sessions.

14. To get a large group organized for handling specific problems, ask them to sit in small groups of four to ten and identify the problems which they think are most important. After ten to thirty minutes (depending on the size of the group; the bigger group needs more time) each group reads off the one problem it feels is crucial. These problems are listed on the blackboard and are grouped together for assignment to several committees. Each person is then asked to select whatever committee he wants to work on. Committee No. 1 meets in this corner of the room, No. 2 in that corner, etc. In this way persons with specific interests are combined into small groups.

15. Patience and a "sober second thought" are necessary ingredients for effective discussion.

16. While these suggestions, properly implemented, will not safeguard against the mere pooling of ignorance or guarantee that the most appropriate action will follow, they will foster a greater degree of what might be called "two-way communication," facilitating the meaningful exchange of ideas.

Bibliography

THE COMMUNITY: ITS STUDY AND ORGANIZATION

BERNARD, JESSIE. *American Community Behavior.* New York: Dryden Press, 1949.

HILLMAN, ARTHUR. *Community Organization and Planning.* New York: Macmillan, 1950.

MERCER, BLAINE E. *The American Community.* New York: Random House, 1956.

PARK, ROBERT E. *Human Communities.* Glencoe: Free Pr., 1952.

POSTON, RICHARD W. *Democracy Is You: A Guide to Citizen Action.* New York: Harper, 1953.

REDFIELD, ROBERT. *The Little Community.* Chicago: Univ. of Chicago Pr., 1955.

WARREN, ROLAND L. *Studying Your Community.* New York: Russell Sage Foundation, 1955.

WIRTH, LOUIS. *Community Life and Social Policy.* Chicago: Univ. of Chicago Pr., 1956.

THE CITY: GROWTH AND FORM

American Sociological Review XXI (February, 1956).

Annals of the American Academy of Political and Social Science, CCCXIV (November, 1957).

BARTHOLEMEW, HARLAND. *Land Uses in American Cities.* Cambridge: Harvard Univ. Pr., 1947.

BEYER, GLENN H. *Housing: A Factual Analysis.* New York: Macmillan, 1958.

BOGUE, DONALD J. "Urbanism in the United States 1950," *The American Journal of Sociology,* LX (March, 1955), 471-486.

BREESE, GERALD, and DOROTHY E. WHITEMAN (eds.). *An Approach to Urban Planning.* Princeton: Princeton Univ. Pr., 1953.

BURGESS, E. W. (ed.). *The Urban Community.* Chicago: Univ. of Chicago Pr., 1926.

CHAPIN, F. STUART, JR. *Urban Land Use Planning.* New York: Harper, 1957.

CHURCHILL, HENRY S. *The City Is the People.* New York: Reynal & Hitchcock, 1945.

FIREY, WALTER. *Land Use in Central Boston.* Cambridge: Harvard Univ. Pr., 1947.

GILMORE, HARLAN W. *Transportation and the Growth of Cities.* Glencoe: Free Pr., 1953.

GIST, NOEL P., and L. A. HALPERT. *Urban Society.* Fourth Edition. New York: Crowell, 1956.

HALLENBECK, WILBUR C. *American Urban Communities.* New York: Harper, 1951.

HATT, PAUL K., and ALBERT J. REISS, (eds.). *Cities and Society: The Revised Reader in Urban Sociology.* Glencoe: Free Pr., 1957.

HILLMAN, ARTHUR, and ROBERT J. CASEY. *Tomorrow's Chicago.* Chicago: Univ. of Chicago Pr., 1953.

MUMFORD, LEWIS. *City Development.* New York: Harcourt Brace, 1945.

MUMFORD, LEWIS. *The Culture of Cities.* New York: Harcourt Brace, 1938.

NELSON, RICHARD L., and FREDERICK T. ASCHMAN. *Real Estate and City Planning.* Englewood Cliffs, N. J.: Prentice-Hall, 1957.

QUEEN, STUART ALFRED, and DAVID BAILEY CARPENTER. *The American City.* New York: McGraw-Hill, 1953.

SCHLESINGER, ARTHUR M. "The City in American History," *Mississippi Valley Historical Review,* XXVII (June, 1940), 43-67.

SCHLESINGER, ARTHUR M. *The Rise of the City, 1878-1898.* New York: Macmillan, 1933.

TUNNARD, CHRISTOPHER, and HENRY HOPE REED. *American Skyline: The Growth and Form of Our Cities and Towns.* New York: Mentor Books, 1956.

VANCE, ROBERT B., and NICHOLAS J. DEMERATH (eds.). *The Urban South.* Chapel Hill: Univ. of N. C. Pr., 1954.

WOODBURY, COLEMAN (ed.). *The Future of Cities and Urban Redevelopment.* Chicago: Univ. of Chicago Pr., 1953.

THE URBAN WAY OF LIFE

The American Journal of Sociology LXII (May, 1957).

BENDIX, REINHARD, and SEYMOUR MARTIN LIPSET. *Class, Status and Power; A Reader in Social Stratification.* Glencoe: Free Pr., 1953.

DRAKE, ST. CLAIR, and HORACE CAYTON. *Black Metropolis.* New York: Harcourt Brace, 1945.

FARIS, R. E. L., and H. WARREN DUNHAM. *Mental Disorders in Urban Areas.* Chicago: Univ. of Chicago Pr., 1939.

FROMM, ERICH. *The Sane Society.* New York: Rinehart, 1955.

HOLLINGSHEAD, AUGUST B. *Elmtown's Youth.* New York: Wiley, 1949.

JANOWITZ, MORRIS. *The Community Press in an Urban Setting.* Glencoe: Free Pr., 1952.

KORNHAUSER, ARTHUR. *Detroit as the People See It: A Survey of Attitudes in an Industrial City.* Detroit: Wayne Univ. Pr., 1952.

LIEPMANN, KATE K. *The Journey to Work.* New York: Oxford Univ. Pr., 1944.

HUNTER, FLOYD. *Community Power Structure: A Study of Decision Makers.* Chapel Hill: Univ. of N. C. Pr., 1953.

LETTS, HAROLD C. (ed.). *Existence Today (Christian Social Responsibility* I). Philadelphia: Muhlenberg Pr., 1957.

MILLS, C. WRIGHT. *White Collar: The American Middle Classes.* New York: Oxford Univ. Pr., 1951.

RIESMAN, DAVID, *et al. The Lonely Crowd: A Study of the Changing American Character.* New Haven: Yale Univ. Pr., 1950.

ROSENBERG, BERNARD, and DAVID MANNING WHITE (eds.). *Mass Culture: The Popular Arts in America.* Glencoe: Free Pr., 1957.

ROSSI, PETER. *Why Families Move: A Study in the Social Psychology of Urban Residential Mobility.* Glencoe: Free Pr., 1955.

SCHMID, CALVIN. *Social Trends in Seattle.* Seattle: Univ. of Wash., 1944.

SHAW, CLIFFORD, and H. D. McKAY. *Juvenile Deliquency and Urban Areas.* Chicago: Univ. of Chicago Pr., 1942.

SHEVKY, ESHREF, and MARYLIN WILLIAMS. *Social Areas of Los Angeles.* Los Angeles: Univ. of Calif. Pr., 1949.

WARNER, LLOYD, and ASSOCIATES. *Democracy in Jonesville.* New York: Harper, 1949.

WARNER, LLOYD, and PAUL S. LUNT. *The Social Life of the Modern Community.* New Haven: Yale Univ. Pr., 1941.

WARNER, LLOYD, and LEO SROLE. *The Social System of American Ethnic Groups.* New Haven: Yale Univ. Pr., 1945.

WHYTE, WILLIAM FOOTE. *Street Corner Society.* Chicago: Univ. of Chicago Pr., 1942.

WHYTE, WILLIAM H., JR. *The Organization Man.* New York: Simon and Schuster, 1956.

WIRTH, LOUIS. *The Ghetto.* Chicago: Univ. of Chicago Pr., 1929.

WIRTH, LOUIS. "Urbanism as a Way of Life," *American Journal of Sociology,* XLIV (July, 1938), 1-24.

THE URBAN CHURCH

ABELL, AARON IGNATIUS. *The Urban Impact on American Protestantism 1869-1900.* Cambridge: Harvard Univ. Pr., 1943.

ABBOTT, SISTER M. MARTINA. *A City Parish Grows and Changes.* Washington: Catholic Univ. of America Pr., 1953.

DOUGLASS, H. PAUL. *The Church in the Changing City.* New York: Harper, 1937.

DOUGLASS, H. PAUL. *One Thousand City Churches.* New York: Doubleday Doran, 1929.

DOUGLASS, H. PAUL. *The St. Louis Church Survey.* New York: Doran, 1924.

DOUGLASS, H. PAUL, and EDMUND DES. BRUNNER. *The Protestant Church as a Social Institution.* New York: Harper, 1935.

FAUSET, A. H. *Black Gods of the Metropolis.* Philadelphia: Univ. of Pa., 1944.

FICHTER, JOSEPH H. *Social Relations in the Urban Parish.* Chicago: Univ. of Chicago Pr., 1954.

FICHTER, JOSEPH H. *Southern Parish: The Dynamics of a City Church.* Chicago: Univ. of Chicago Pr., 1951.

FOSSELMAN, DAVID HAROLD. *Transitions in the Development of a Downtown Parish.* Washington: Catholic Univ. of America Pr., 1952.

HERBERG, WILL. *Protestant-Catholic-Jew: An Essay in American Religious Sociology*. New York: Doubleday, 1956.

HOOVER, ROBERT C., and EVERETT L. PERRY. *Church and City Planning*. New York: Department of the Urban Church, Division of Home Missions, N.C.C.C.U.S.A., 1955.

HOTCHKISS, WESLEY AKIN. *Areal Patterns of Religious Institutions in Cincinnati*. Chicago: Department of Geography, Univ. of Chicago, 1950.

KINCHELOE, S. C. *The American City and Its Church*. New York: Friendship Pr., 1938.

LEIFFER, MURRAY H. *The Effective City Church* (Revised Edition). New York: Abingdon Pr., 1955.

MAY, HENRY F. *Protestant Churches and Industrial America*. New York: Harper, 1949.

MILLER, KENNETH D. *Man and God in the City*. New York: Friendship Pr., 1954.

NIEBUHR, H. RICHARD. *The Social Sources of Denominationalism*. New York: Holt, 1929.

POPE, LISTON. *The Kingdom Beyond Caste*. New York: Friendship Pr., 1957.

POPE, LISTON. *Millhands and Preachers*. New Haven: Yale Univ. Pr., 1942.

POPE, LISTON. "Religion and the Class Structure," *Annals of the American Academy of Political and Social Science*, CCLVI (March, 1948), 84-91.

PRESBYTERIAN CHURCH IN THE U.S.A., Special Committee of the Board of National Missions. *Report on the Study of the Inner City*. New York: Board of National Missions, Presbyterian Church in the U.S.A., 1956.

SANDERSON, ROSS W. *The Church Serves the Changing City*. New York: Harper, 1955.

SANDERSON, ROSS W. (ed.). *Toward Better City Churches*. New York· Department of the Urban Church, Division of Home Missions, N.C.C.C.U.S.A., 1955.

SHIPPEY, FREDERICK A. *Church Work in the City*. New York: Abingdon Pr., 1952.

SKLARE, MARSHALL. *Conservative Judaism: An American Religious Movement*. Glencoe: Free Pr., 1955.

UNDERWOOD, KENNETH WILSON. *Protestant and Catholic Religious and Social Interaction in an Industrial Community.* Boston: Beacon Pr., 1957.

YINGER, J. MILTON. *Religion in the Struggle for Power.* Durham, N. C.: Duke Univ. Pr., 1946.

YINGER, J. MILTON. *Religion, Society and the Individual.* New York: Macmillan, 1957.

Index

Type used in this book
Body, 10 on 13 Caledonia
Display, Tempo
Paper: White Spring Grove E. F.